UNSTUCK

UNSTUCK

How to Break Through Writer's Block,
Find Your Voice and Get into the
College of your Dreams

Gabrielle Glancy

ONEIRIC
PRESS

Oneiric Press
www.oneiricpress.org

Book Layout ©2019 Tracy R. Atkins
Book Cover by Tanja Prokop

Unstuck/ Gabrielle Glancy. —1st ed.
ISBN Paperback: 978-0-9973529-7-9
ISBN Ebook: 978-0-9973529-8-6

Ever and always, with deep gratitude and respect, this book is dedicated to my students, who have trusted me with their stories and with the journey it took to find and articulate them.

And to my mother, whose wild imagination, brilliant command of the language, and faith in me, helped me unearth my voice, and find my own unique path in life.

You can't think yourself out of a writing block; you have to write yourself out of a thinking block. — John Rogers

One must still have chaos in oneself to be able to give birth to a dancing star. — Nietzsche

CONTENTS

PREFACE

Midway upon the road of [my] life I found myself within a dark wood, for the right way had been missed. Ah! how hard a thing it is to tell what this wild and rough and dense wood was, which in thought renews the fear!... I cannot well recount how I entered it, so full was I of slumber at that point where I abandoned the true way... I looked on high, and saw its shoulders clothed already with the rays of the planet that leadeth men aright along every path. Then was the fear a little quieted which in the lake of my heart had lasted through the night that I passed so piteously.

Dante's *Inferno*

Had I not myself come upon a roadblock in my own life, my own "dark wood," I might not have written UNSTUCK at all.

Fellow writer, dear friend and spiritual warrior Dave Richo, seeing me floundering, emailed me the following passage from a book called *Bewilderments* by Avivah Gottleib Zornberg.

Between Egypt and the Holy Land, the wilderness intervenes... the brief interlude suddenly and tragically swells to deathly proportions.

What is the nature of this interim space, so terribly extended?... This is not simply a walking surface for the traveling people, but a quicksand ready to consume human bodies... [Those who do fall] "vanish" from the human landscape, into the netherworld: the hungry maw of the earth has removed them from the surface on which human acts are played out. Nothingness has triumphed over being.

I found this passage comforting, believe it or not. *Then was the fear a little quieted... in the lake of my heart.*

There seemed a name for what I was feeling, and/or at least someone out there felt it too. And of course, we know how the story ends. Those who were lost find their "true way" to the Promised Land.

I recognized the feelings I was having as a kind of "stuckness," and saw with my whole body that these feelings were very similar to those I had felt when I had suffered from writer's block.

I suddenly experienced an even greater empathy for my students. It had been a long time since I was unable to access the voice of my inner world. Perhaps I had grown complacent?

But now, faced with health challenges, feeling at a crossroads in my career, I had a renewed appreciation for the feeling of being blocked as a writer.

And thus was born the idea for this book.

"This terrible image (of nothingness triumphing over being)," Zornberg goes on to say, haunts the reader. As she describes, lost in a pathless wood, the writer feels disoriented, panicky even. Where will one find sustenance, or in this case meaning, in a landscape indifferent and even hostile to human endeavor?

Are there no markings to indicate a mapping of this blank space? Frustration mounts. Fear. "No human steps have trod this sand, it stares back at the traveler indifferently—pathless, *bewildering* to the human imagination. A kind of horror besets the mind…"

This horror that Zornberg describes — that pathless wood (Robert Frost), that heart of darkness (Joseph Conrad), we know it deeply and well (though perhaps not fully consciously.) We have all already been there — otherwise we would not know to be so afraid of it — and we do not wish to go back.

A blank page…

An empty space…

Suddenly the bottom falls out. There we are, naked, helpless, unable to make our cries understood.

This moment describes the moment before becoming, from the darkness and void, to light and being.

This happened to us already, at conception, and then again at birth.

The curse, or blessing, of human birth, of course, is that the "horror" of this experience is erased from conscious memory. Most of us cannot recall the moment we were thrust out of our homeland into the desert of the world, though the felt sense of the experience lies deep within us.

Just as the Israelites of the story left their home to escape slavery, our moment of birth is the moment we are cast out and yet freed.

Here is the birth of selfhood, and its twin sister, loneliness.

Finally we are free, but unfortunately, we are lost. Or to look at it another way, before all beginning, all options are open to us.

Whatever brought us to the brink of creation, whatever inner resources and strokes of good fortune carried us through — we do not even have any previous, or at least conscious, memory of having once survived the "original" breakthrough to refer to and rely on.

Yet these moments that haunt us — the loneliness, the terror, the feeling of being lost in the wilderness — are the essential birthplace, the primal and necessary seedbed of the writer, (who wants nothing more than to sound her barbaric yawp over the rooftops of the world, and in so doing, find at least one mysterious other who can understand her, and thus help her find her way.)

You know how wide the chasm of nothingness can open when faced with a blank page, or the seemingly unbridgeable transition from one-only-barely-understood thought to another.

There lies the heart of darkness, or light, depending on how you look at it.

I have visited this wild and uncharted territory, this wilderness of inner experience and desire for outer expression, more times than I can count, and I have lived to talk about it.

I thought at points that if it didn't kill me, I should kill myself!

Surely you know what I mean — the crumpled pages, false starts, self-abnegation… It's enough to silence even the strongest among us.

But then, as if by some miracle, something gives… or appears. "There is a crack though which the light gets in," as Leonard Cohen describes it.

Suddenly, a thought creates itself. It multiplies and divides. The life that brims in each thought overflows until it becomes another, and then another.

Over and over, this has happened to me in my writing life.

Somehow in my process working with students, I am able to locate and help facilitate the birth of ideas. Again and again, I have helped students overcome writer's block and realize their dreams.

To read a poem, to behold a work of art, is to witness breakthrough.

From the void there came light…

Life cannot exist without breakthrough. A blade of grass breaks through the soil. The chick cracks open the egg. The baby's head crowns. Even single-celled organisms break out of their membranes and one becomes two.

And yet it is the nature of nature to keep its mysteries and obscure its origins.

Therein lies the fundamental difficulty in teaching someone how to create something from nothing, out of thin air, as the painter Paul Klee describes:

Everything vanishes around me and works are formed as if out of the void. Ripe, graphic fruits fall off. My hand has become the obedient instrument of a remote will.

Out of thin air? Something from nothing? How can this happen?

You cannot know from whence your words will come. It doesn't really matter.

That is where faith comes in.

To midwife this process has been the task of my lifetime. I am honored and moved to have lived long enough and worked hard enough to have a few things to say about it that may be helpful.

INTRODUCTION

There you are. Face to face with a blank page, prompts pulled up on the screen, fingers poised above the keyboard, ready to begin…

Yikes! What do you do now?

Your college admissions essay is one of the most important pieces of writing you will ever be required to write in your whole life (not to make you more nervous than you are, but it's true). And yet you probably have no idea how to go about writing one of these essays (which is why I have a job!)

You have likely written plenty of five-paragraph analytical essays, but a narrative personal statement — what is that?

Narrative means story. The College Admissions essay is a story essay — one that tells a story about who you are, what's important to you, how you face adversity, what kind of contribution you are likely to make, to the community you are about to enter, and eventually, to the world.

It is the means by which the Admissions Committee (Ad Com) "meets" you before being able to shake your hand. Since these days very few schools do personal interviews, your essays are often the only place in which you can really *show* them what you're made of.

Perhaps it will calm you to know that writing is difficult for everyone.

Writing under pressure is even more difficult.

But knowing that doesn't really help you write, does it?

I have been a teacher of writing all my life. My quest has been to help students find their voice, and in so doing, find themselves, or sometimes the other way around.

Having worked in admissions at three different colleges and universities, once as an Admissions Director, I know firsthand what it takes to grab the attention of the Ad Com. This is exactly what you must do to get into the college(s) of your dreams. All else being equal, your essay(s) will tip the scales in your favor, or not.

Out of the pile of boring, cardboardy, try-too-hard essays, yours must shine like a brilliant star.

To get in, you must stand out.

That's a lot of pressure on a process that requires let-go to perform.

Actually, finding your voice is a bit of a misnomer. You already *have* your voice. It's in there somewhere. It's just a matter of being free enough to uncover it.

While this book is focused on students writing their college essays, it can be used by anyone who, face-to-face with a blank page, encounters writer's block.

The mainstay of my method is the Free Write, emphasis on FREE. And my motto: "You must get lost in order to get found."

It's not easy getting free. I often have to coax students out of their straitjackets — the five-paragraph essay with all its trappings or their preconceived notion of how things are *supposed to sound*.

I have not met a single student, however, who to the very end resists freedom. All of them — I would have to say 100% — find their way out of the labyrinth their training has entrapped them in or the one which they themselves have created.

The taste of freedom is sweet.

Yet how many people would thank you for asking them to take the most stressful moment of their lives and deliberately make a mess out of it?

That's what the free write asks you to do. Let your hair down. Let 'er rip. Don't look back and don't worry about the future. Just write whatever comes to mind.

The moment inevitably arrives when you have to do something with all that mess.

How do you find order in the chaos?

There are some tricks. Be patient. I will teach them to you.

Making order out of chaos is a lot easier than creating something out of nothing, under time-pressure, having no idea what to do.

But first, let's see if any of these "blocks" ring a bell for you.

Nerves

When faced with a piece of writing this important, it's easy to freeze. Just the thought of writing may make you nervous. Does everyone feel this way?

Narrative Personal Statement? What's That?

You have probably been trained to write in one form, and one form only — the analytical essay. Perhaps you have written a reflection now and again to the tune of *Tell us about your summer vacation.* The college admissions essay, however, is a narrative personal statement. How do you write one of those? What even is it?

This Sounds Dumb

You start and stop, start and stop. "This sounds stupid," you say to yourself. Or, "How shall I begin?" But editing your writing while you're in the process of writing is a killjoy. You have to refrain from doing that. In addition, even though you've been taught to write an introduction first, it's the worst place to start writing. How can you introduce something before you know what you want to say?

Telling Them What You Think They Want to Hear

What they really want is an authentic expression of who you are, the challenges you have faced, how you have dealt with adversity, what floats your boat. As soon as you start puffing yourself up to try to sound appealing, you're sunk. The most powerful essays I've read are those that tell a real story about a real person facing real-life circumstances. You must find your story and tell it from your heart.

Nothing Big Has Happened to Me. I Don't Have a Topic. What Should I Write About?

Just as everyone has a voice, everyone has a story, even if the story is the anxiety you are facing in embarking on this journey. You don't need a topic to begin writing. You need to begin writing to find a topic.

This book seeks to address the anxiety that inevitably comes with writing. It addresses the "inner game of writing." And I hope it sets you free.

What This Book is Not

UNSTUCK is not a step-by-step how-to guide to writing college essays from beginning to end. I wrote that book already. It's called The Art of the College Essay.

In a sense, UNSTUCK is a detail of a very large and complex painting of the creative process. In this book, I zoom in on one particular moment — the moment in which you are called to break through the silence and sound your "barbaric yawp" into the world.

"This process doesn't have to be learned; we already know it. All that is needed it to unlearn those habits which interfere with it and then to just let it happen," writes Timothy Gallwey in *The Inner Game of Tennis.*

What This Book Is About

I decided a long time ago that one day I wanted to assemble all the tricks, strategies and techniques I have used to help students achieve writing breakthroughs.

A few years ago, I started asking my students to describe their writing process to me, where they got stuck, and what helped them break through, with the idea that one day I would put it all in a book that could be used to help students, coming up the ranks, write their college essays.

That book is the one before you.

The goal of the book is liberation and freedom. I hope it will give you a leg up over the wall, inspire you to come up with ideas you never knew you had, and help you access your own inner and unique voice.

My hope is it will demystify the writing process while at the same time sprinkling it with magic dust.

This doesn't have to be a book you read from start to finish.

You can touch down wherever you like. Read a sample essay. See what the writer of that essay has to say about what happened to him or her in the process of writing it.

The highlighted sections contain tips, tricks and reflections on the writing process and on feeling blocked. These alone can provide inspiration.

In some cases, I have chosen to comment, alongside the writer, about what I remember or did or saw as he or she was writing it.

Sometimes, I just let the writers or the essays speak for themselves.

I hope UNSTUCK will be true to its name and help you to find a freedom in writing you may not otherwise have known, and get *unstuck*.

I want you to feel as I do that you can confidently face any writing task you undertake with ease and success. I don't want you to shy away from writing. I want you to leave this experience saying: Bring it on!

CHAPTER 1

The Inner Game of Writing

I started playing tennis when I was eleven. By the time I was thirteen, I was teaching tennis to adults. I had natural ability. I was fast (though short), strong (built more like Serena Williams than like Sharapova before Serena made "thick" seem cool), good eye-hand coordination, and I loved the game. I also had unusual stamina — I could outlast anyone on the court. (I only found out recently, after doing a DNA test, that I have the genes of a "Power Elite Athlete.") By all accounts, I should have become a world-class tennis player. That's what my coaches told me. That's what they hoped for!

Unfortunately, I didn't like competition.

I lost to players I should have beaten. And (mostly) beat players to whom I should have lost.

You can't get anywhere playing this way. One step forward, one step back. It amounts to, well, walking in place.

Partly, I didn't have a "killer instinct."

But it was more than that.

Tennis is a mental game. What it takes to hit that little fuzzy neon-yellow ball with a racket no bigger than your head, across the court, over a net exactly three feet high, into a box the size of your kitchen — it's almost unfathomable.

You need ridiculous amounts of concentration, a lot of skill — and unflagging confidence.

One moment of self-doubt, one negative thought, one tiny fleck of fear — the ball is over the fence.

I hit a lot of balls over the fence!

I also hit a lot of winners and could rally for hours.

But every thirty or forty shots, I became possessed by an alien. My wrist would quiver, I'd have a "jolt," and all bets were off. The ball would tip the end of my racket and head for the stars.

It was unpredictable, always a shock — and downright humiliating.

My opponent was as startled as I. There she goes again, another wild ball. Mouths would fly open. Even the umpires couldn't believe it.

You can still win matches and be successful even if you have "the jolt," by the way, but only if the crazy phenomenon that came to be my trademark doesn't happen at break or match point.

If I knew then what I know now, I wouldn't have worried about it at all. In fact, it wouldn't have been a problem. I would have come to accept and account for it.

I would have trusted it was going to happen. I would have prepared for it in my psyche. I would have taken "the jolt" in stride and pressed forward for the win. I might even have used it to my advantage. After all, when out of the blue the ball flies into the crowd like a home run — that kind of unexpected wildness — it throws everybody off!

In time, way after my problematic tennis career was over, I came to recognize "the jolt" as part of my everyday life. Every fifth time I shake out a Vitamin C from the jar, for example, brown-gray capsules end up flying everywhere. I cannot be trusted with a cup of hot tea.

I was young when I played competitive tennis. I didn't know or trust myself like I do now.

Back then, I spent many sleepless nights before important matches fearing the inevitable. I would hold my arm out to see if it was shaking. I would stretch out, try to stay limber, practice staying calm. I could feel the potential for "the jolt" like a coiled spring in my right wrist about to snap. I was almost twitching with the possibility.

One day, my practice partner gave me a book. "Read it," he said. "I think it's gonna help you a lot."

That book was *The Inner Game of Tennis,* by Timothy Gallwey. I not only read the book, I slept with it under my pillow. *The Inner Game of Tennis* became my bible, Gallwey's words my mantra:

> *There is a far more natural and effective process for learning and doing almost anything than most of us realize. It is similar to the process we all used, but soon forget, as we learned to walk and talk. It uses the intuitive capabilities of the mind and both the right and left hemispheres of the brain. This process doesn't have to learned; we already know it. All that is needed it to unlearn those habits which interfere with it and then to just let it happen.*

I started playing competitive tennis the year that book came out, 1974. I see now Gallwey was ahead of his time.

In *The Inner Game of Tennis*, he speaks about ideas that would later come into fashion in books on peak performance, books about getting into "the zone."

At the time, though, the "inner" aspect of *The Inner Game of Tennis* was kind of radical.

The player of the inner game comes to value **the art of relaxed concentration** *above all other skills; he discovers a true basis for self-confidence; and he learns that the secret to winning any game lies in not trying too hard.*

I could well have called this book "The Inner Game of Writing."

There are a lot of books out there on how to execute "the strokes" to write a winning college essay.

They tell you how to structure your essay, how to spice it up, how to refine and revise it — these things are important — and I will speak to and about them in this book as well.

But all these books leave out one essential element: the mental challenge of writing — not just a college essay — but anything!

No amount of guidance focusing on the external elements of the craft can help a writer explore her own mind, let alone break through a state of "stuckness."

And to be honest, being blocked seems to be universal — and fundamental — when it comes to writing. I'm not sure whether we're born with difficulty writing. Or it's because of how writing is taught in school.

I have a feeling it's a bit of both.

Tennis is one of the most challenging sports out there. Anyone will tell you that.

Writing is even more difficult than tennis.

Because writing is mental in its very nature, entirely relying on the workings of the mind, it's even more challenging to put the (thinking) mind aside in order to be able to do it.

And yet, though it may seem counterintuitive, in a certain way, to write well, to find your flow, you must put the mind to sleep.

The many ways to do this, and how these principles apply to writing, is what will be explored in the chapters ahead.

CHAPTER 2

The Trance-like State

*And if there is one more thing that I must say to you, it is this:
Don't think that the person who is trying to comfort you now lives
untroubled among the simple and quiet words that sometimes give
you pleasure. His life has much trouble and sadness, and remains
far behind yours. Were it otherwise, he would never have been able
to find those words.* — Rilke, *Letters to a Young Poet*

Right now, I would be wearing a white lab coat with a
stethoscope around my neck, were it not for my own experience
with writer's block. But of course, had there been no impasse,
there would have been no breakthrough.

I struggled for many years with my own writing. The moment
I got an assignment, I would panic! Sometimes my writer's block
took the form of dumbfoundedness. Suddenly, all thoughts would
leave my mind. The sinkhole would open and I would fall right in
it.

Sometimes I would start a sentence, and start it again a
hundred times, trying to perfect it before I even knew what I
wanted to express. "In Shakespeare's *Hamlet,* written by

Shakespeare…" "Hamlet, the main characters of Shakespeare's play *Hamlet*…" The plane would crash before ever getting off the ground.

I had a teacher once who called this exercise in futility "manicuring a corpse." You haven't said much of anything and you're already trying to make it perfect.

In fact, my whole career as a writer was born out of a terrible case of writer's block. It was why I was a premed English major. Math and science came easily to me, and even though I wanted more than anything else to become a writer, I just couldn't write. It looked like I was destined for medical school. What a dilemma! I was so torn at one point that I actually sought the help of a career counselor, a very kind man with straight blond hair that came to points on his forehead, Dr. David Cotton. I remember he had me role play a scene in which, wearing my white lab coat and stethoscope, I enter the examining room, introduce myself, and shake the patient's hand.

"Good morning. I'm Dr. Glancy."

"Then what do you say?" Dr. Cotton had a very serious look of concentration on his face.

"So where ya from?"

"I don't think you should be a doctor," he said, shaking his head. "Remember, the patient is sick?"

I'm sure Dr. Cotton was right.

My next questions would have been, "Do you remember your dreams? What have you read lately? What's your favorite movie?"

Though I wish I did have a doctor who asked me questions such as these, my sensibility probably wouldn't fly in med school.

Luckily, I met Tom Vogler at The University of California at Santa Cruz, who taught Romantic Poetry. He told me in slightly different words what I'm going to tell you. For that class we had to write a paper a week. My first one — excuse the French —

sucked. It was a perfectly formed corpse. Dead. Boring. Totally uninspired. And I suffered writing it just as I had done with my assignments all the years before.

Then we read Coleridge's *Kubla Kahn* which he told us was written in and about an opium induced state of delirium.

> *So twice five miles of fertile ground*
> *With walls and towers were girdled round;*
> **And from this chasm**, *with ceaseless turmoil seething,*
> *As if this earth in fast thick pants were breathing,*
> **A mighty fountain momently was forced:**
> *Amid whose swift half-intermitted burst*
> **Huge fragments vaulted like rebounding hail...**

"Write from that place," Vogler said. "And keep writing. Don't stop. However you want to do it, get yourself into a trance."

I remember one Sunday morning — each paper was due on Monday — climbing through the ground floor window of a locked classroom building to find a quiet place to en-trance myself.

That particular morning — it couldn't have been more than six a.m. — just as I put my left foot over the window ledge, I saw my professor, Harry Berger, tootling down the path between redwoods in a reveal-all Speedo sporting the good ol' stars and stripes on his way to the nearby pool. He waved. I waved back. I'm not sure who looked more sheepish.

Touching my toes into "Alph [abet]," sacred river, while immersed/submerged in what I have come to call "the trance-like state," the words started to flow, "as if this earth in fast thick pants were breathing," until "A mighty fountain momently was forced!"

I was free.

I'm not sure exactly how I got there, to be honest. I only know I did.

Perhaps it was from the sheer volume of writing we had to do for that class. You couldn't be too precious if you had to hand in a paper a week. Or maybe it was a kind of contact-trance from reading all that Coleridge, Wordsworth and Keats.

I know for sure that reading is one of the great muses. It always has been for me. I can hardly pick up a book without wanting to write one.

Whatever the reason, the experience was profound.

I felt the change in my body. I would describe it as being taken into, or spontaneously finding an "en-trance" into the aura of light or river of words, whatever you want to call it, carried along by an invisible, clear stream of unselfconscious... I guess you would call it thought?

Gallwey, in *The Inner Game of Tennis,* describes it as "a pure light energy whose power is to make events knowable, just as an electric light makes objects visible." In an effort to describe the indescribable as I am attempting to do here, he goes on to say: "Consciousness could be called the light of lights because it is by its light that all other lights become visible."

I am amazed that once I had felt it and recognized the feeling, once I had embodied it and brought it to consciousness, I never lost it.

I could call it back in an instant — sometimes with the help of techniques I will offer you here — and sometimes just by recalling the feelings and re-entering, as if it were a parallel universe, the trance-like state I had come upon that day. Then I let myself be taken down the river for as long, I suppose, as I believed and trusted the river would take me.

The feeling is much like that in my flying dreams. Often, I am hovering, like a glider, in the middle of a large room. Sometimes I am soaring above the mountains; sometimes just taking off between the trees. There's no flapping of arms, no jet pack, no propeller. As long as I have faith, I can stay aloft.

Let the demons gnash and writhe in the dark pools of fear somewhere down there below the surface of the earth.

Doubt

And by the way, everything in life is writable about if you have the outgoing guts to do it, and the imagination to improvise. The worst enemy to creativity is self-doubt. — Sylvia Plath

Once you have seen the light, your job is to keep your eye on the prize. In a sense you must hold the feeling-image of yourself entering the trance-like state.

You must do what my student Niko describes here in his college essay on breaking through his fear of becoming a lifeguard:

Should I talk to my boss and tell her I'm not cut out for this? Suddenly, I saw an image of myself taking action. I pictured myself diving into the pool for an unconscious child. Grabbing his bloated body. His parents watching. Beginning compressions on his cold chest. The look of his unconscious face. What if he doesn't make it? But I wasn't going to quit. Yes, I thought. I'm ready to accept the duty of saving lives.

As one technique to enter the trance-like state, Gallwey suggests you "listen to the ball."

When I write, I hear the ball, as it were, even though I am light years from the tennis court sitting in my well-worn ergonomic chair. It is like the whirr of shooting stars as I follow on my path through the Milky Way, the flow of the river that carries me, the music of the wind in the trees.

"Listen to the ball."

CHAPTER 3

A Voice in the Wilderness

Had I asked Aaron to write an essay about how he found himself, I am sure he would have gotten stuck. That's a big question to put to a seventeen-year-old sitting in front of his computer.

I'm not sure I myself could answer that question as eloquently as Aaron did in one 650-word essay, especially if I attempted to write it from start to finish.

You'd have your topic — how you found yourself. But how would you go about writing on it?

Locating moments and free writing on them is the best way to find your topic. Aaron didn't know this was his topic until he wrote the essay, by the way. Here is his final essay. I will provide commentary on the process in the pages that follow.

Many players started weeping, some got angry, I simply put my head down. This was our beloved coach's last season. We stood in a line, waiting to give him a hug before we officially said goodbye. When my turn came, he took me in and started crying.

Two summers before, he was just my coach. Now he was my friend.

Not that long ago, I was a different Aaron. That Aaron was not the person that I am today. It was as if he had strayed from the trail and found himself lost in the forest. The point guard would be dribbling the ball up the court. All of a sudden, I would stop running. I felt my stomach tighten up; I put my head down. I felt alone, like the only person in a wooden box. The vibrations of each dribble rang in my head. *What's wrong with you?*

"AARON!" I looked up to see the ball whiz through my hands and a sub jogging in to replace me.

It was these moments in which I thought about quitting. I became afraid even to go to practices. Anxiety would build in me, then doubt, then fear. I had experienced this before, during conditioning. But my mind was healthy then, I could persevere. The summer of my illness was different. I saw no end and no purpose. Where before I felt strength building inside of me, now it seemed to be seeping out.

Sitting on the bench, looking out at my team on the court, I longed to be able to compete with the grace and ease that I saw my teammates possessed. It seemed like it was a past life in which I could do anything productive with a basketball. I was once a man on a mission. I longed to feel that power again.

There was a moment during a game, a timeout actually, where my beloved coach called me out like never before. "Aaron! When are you gonna step up and guard somebody!? They're going at you every single time! They've found the fish, Aaron. YOU'RE THE FISH!"

In that instant, I felt like crying. I wanted to walk over to the bench, plop down in a chair and weep. If I didn't have to ride back home with my dad that night, I might have bawled my eyes out like I wanted to.

There was no single day that I can point out, no one moment in which I recovered. It seemed like I began to gain my strength back without noticing it. I do remember discovering a new lens through which I could live a normal life. I forced myself to eat a little more each day and I pushed myself just a little harder on the court. Over time, I could play as I wanted, free from the demons of my illness. I looked for those happy moments, because if I could find them, I could live through this summer.

Eventually, my morning eggs started to taste good; the backyard garden seemed pretty again and waking up brought hope for the coming day. That summer was the longest summer of my life, but I made it through.

I don't know how I got better actually. Somehow there were mysterious forces at work.

When I was nine years old, I had a similar experience. The Dodgers were on the brink of defeat. In desperation I ran upstairs and grabbed my prayer book. I started to sing in Hebrew, making sure to pronounce every word correctly and hit every note with pristine accuracy. Suddenly, in what seemed like an instant, the tide turned and the Dodgers won 3-2. They seemed to pull the victory out of nowhere. Before that I was a kid who didn't believe — in the power of prayer, the supernatural or even miracles. Now I wondered if my prayers had affected the outcome of the game. I knew that I would never know the answer, so I decided to believe that they had.

"You know, you could be a rabbi," my rabbi had said as he pulled me in under the arc during my *Bar Mitzvah*. I almost knew he was going to say that. Maybe he saw something in me that I already sensed was there.

But it was not until that summer that I discovered who I really was — a believer, not necessarily a believer in God or miracles or anything like that, but a believer in the power of people, the power within me. I found hope and happiness in the darkest of places. I pushed through an immovable wall and uncovered my belief in myself. Had I not found that strength I would not be the Aaron I am today. Had I not been through the wilderness, I would not be me.

I had asked Aaron to find five significant moments in his life in which he went into an experience one person and came out slightly, or more than slightly, changed.

He free wrote on the moment his coach hugged him, the time he flubbed a basketball game and felt ashamed, a period of unexplainable illness he underwent from which he miraculously recovered, a moment of praying for his favorite team to win, seeing them pull it out of the hat and wondering if his prayers had been answered, and finally the moment his rabbi told him he could one day become a rabbi himself.

His free write was well over 3,000 words long. His moments were not written in the order they appear in this essay and the conclusion was not that he found his way in the wilderness. There was no conclusion.

Rather, once he had done the free writes — each one on a different moment — he read what he had written to figure out what he was trying to say.

Like a photograph placed in a developer, the image of the whole began to take shape before his/our very eyes.

What does the basketball game have to do with being a rabbi? I asked him. How does being sick fit into this? Why was that hug from your coach so important?

I asked him questions.

Little by little, the tide turned and Aaron began to see where the flow was leading him. He saw that each of his moments was somehow related.

Was it an accident? A coincidence?

It turned out that all of his moments had come from the same place. "Somehow there were mysterious forces at work."

In the process of writing this essay, Aaron "found hope and happiness in the darkest of places. [He] pushed through an immovable wall and uncovered [his] belief in himself."

But he had to go through the "wilderness" that is *the writing process* to do so.

Had he been worried in advance about how it was all going to fit together and turn out, he might have panicked.

And his panic might have led him to rely on what he had been taught. He might have attempted to write an introduction first — the introduction to who knows what — and to follow it with body paragraphs that supported the "thesis."

I was lost and now I'm found?

In fact, he could have started the essay from many other places than where he started it, and it still would have worked.

His first line could have been: "The Dodgers were on the brink of defeat."

Or perhaps, "They found the fish, Aaron. YOU'RE the fish!"

Or even, "I was once a man on a mission."

Once you have a Free Write, you can look it over to find a good first sentence.

This way of doing things — choosing a lead sentence from the six hundred you've written — may seem counterintuitive, but actually it's much easier than generating a first line out of thin air — and trying to write an essay in a straight line from there.

It is in the process of writing that Aaron found his way, and I suppose, himself.

To do this, however, is to trust the unknown for, as Donald Barthelme writes, *"Without the possibility of having the mind move in unanticipated directions, there would be no invention."*

Aaron got into Columbia University where last I heard he was studying political science and/or biology. It remains to be seen whether he ever becomes a rabbi.

CHAPTER 4

Thing Two and Thing One

These things will not bite you
They want to have fun
Then, out of the box came
Thing Two and Thing One.
— Dr. Seuss, *The Cat in the Hat*

To return for a moment to my thwarted tennis career: the most devastating consequence of the jolt was that though it may have started as physical/neurological, after a time, because it was so disturbing and unpredictable, it *became* mental. I began to perseverate over it, became self-conscious because of it — I came to fear it.

In that case, as I described, I could potentially have separated the mental aspects of the jolt from the physical and just let it be what it was — a momentary, unexplainable, random loss of control.

With writing, it's a bit different, and somewhat more complicated.

Words are formed in the mind. The body is only a vehicle for transmitting words. The mind uses the mechanics of the larynx, the pencil or the keyboard, to bring itself into manifest form — but, as I mention in Chapter 1, writing is in essence a mental activity.

And yet, just as in tennis, the mind can get in the way.

While it may be possible to divorce mind from body, how would you divorce mind from mind?

You may recall in *The Cat in the Hat* that when Thing Two and Thing One — the mischievous, energetic twins — are let out of the box, all hell breaks loose.

"They fly kites and wreak havoc, knocking over pots and stools and pictures and dragging around the children's mother's new gown."

They trip over toys, knock over tables, nearly jolt the fish out of its bowl, and create so much chaos that even the fish is afraid of what will happen when Mother gets home.

"'He should not be here,' said the fish in the pot. 'He should not be here when your mother is not.'"

The fish, like a goody two shoes, has fear. He warns the kids not to trust Thing Two and Thing One.

That's very different from the playful, mischievous, power-packed duo who have been let out of the box.

The fish is like the thinking mind. We will call the fish "the critic." You could also call him the super-ego, the thought-police, the killjoy, the superintendent of writer's block. The critic is responsible for making sure everything is in order. It concerns itself with rules, organization, grammar, punctuation and spelling, sequence of ideas, editing and proofreading. It is by nature *critical*. The fish says things like: "That's stupid. Why did you write that? How do you intend to organize this? What a mess! You'd better clean up before Mother gets home!"

The fish, though important, needs to be kept in check.

Thing Two and Thing One, we will call the creator. This is the part of the brain that is imaginative, non-linear, fractal-like and free. And note, when out of the box, the creator packs the punch of two. And they are named out of order: Thing Two and Thing One.

Even though you need both sides of the brain, the critic will try to rain on your parade.

On the other hand, if you never let the critic have a say, if Thing Two and Thing One rule the world, it would be total anarchy and chaos.

So you need them both. The trick is to keep them apart for as long as possible.

I often illustrate what I am describing here by telling students about my experience snorkeling in a mangrove river.

Mangroves have their roots in the water. When you look down, you see fish swimming in and out of the roots.

But you cannot just look down when you're snorkeling in a mangrove river. You must also look up and ahead. You must watch for stray branches, boulders, sticks and leaves.

The ideal position to be in while snorkeling in a mangrove river is with half your mask below the surface of the water, the other half above.

This is a perfect metaphor for that "split" of the mind to which Gallwey and many other philosophers/thinkers refer — the conscious and the unconscious mind, the egoic and non-egoic mind, Thing Two and Thing One.

In the optimal state, you are aware and awake, on one hand. On the other, the critic has somehow, temporarily, been put to sleep.

CHAPTER 5

Write First, Think Later

"Don't bend; don't water it down; don't try to make it logical; don't edit your own soul according to the fashion. Rather, follow your most intense obsessions mercilessly."— Franz Kafka

The inner critic causes anxiety. And writing and anxiety don't mix. Once anxiety enters the picture, creativity skulks away and hides in a corner.

I think it's Freud who said: "Anxiety is the great narrower."

Anxiety makes you contract, freeze, get small and afraid.

But how do you avoid anxiety in a high stakes game like trying to get into college?

Beginning early, and allowing yourself time and space, helps. Create an opportunity to invite in the muse — a moment when you feel like you might be able to "listen to the ball," or even when you hear the ball calling. Sometimes it will. You have to jump on these moments, even if this happens in the wee hours of the night.

I have often, grudgingly, gotten out of bed to write down a thought when I have sensed it is important.

I have always been glad I did so.

In addition to moments of opportunity, you also need an expanse of time.

Except in rare cases, writing takes time. True, there are instances in which you sit down and write a brilliant essay from start to finish all in one go. But you can't count on it.

If you start early, at least you eliminate one of writing's worst enemies — the pressure of deadlines almost too close to meet.

But the truth is, even if you have all the time in the world, writing still seems to stir up anxiety.

Perhaps the most important element of what I'm describing involves recognizing whether or not you're "in the zone" at any given moment. If you are, write, and keep writing, as long as the river takes you. If you're not, you have two choices: You can try to *get* into the zone yourself using methods I describe in the following chapters. Or you can get up and make a sandwich.

How do you put the "thinking mind" aside and allow the creative part of yourself to come out of the box?

I have found in my own writing, and in my work with students, that you can't go at this directly.

To quote Gallwey: "Focus is not achieved by *staring at* [or thinking] hard about something. . . Natural focus occurs when the mind is interested."

It seems you almost have to trick yourself into letting the mind go. The critic is devious and protean, a shapeshifter. You cannot really outsmart or outrun it. You kind of have to distract it. A spirit of play is one of the ways to do this — let Thing One and Thing Two out of the box.

Don't worry about deadlines, rules, grammar — these create an environment inhospitable to the creative mind/impulse.

Play, on the other hand, is one of creativity's most reliable wellsprings.

In my work with students who are stuck, I don't say: Come on. What's wrong with you? Can't you just start writing?

Rather, I turn writing into a game.

It's worth noting here the difficulty in deconstructing a process with the thinking mind that does not involve the thinking mind. That's like hearing the sound of one hand clapping. It's a built-in conundrum.

In my experience, play is the best way to create opportunities for a chance or accidental moment of inspiration to occur. Once the words start flowing, I keep quiet until the stream runs dry. At that point, when the student has written as much as they can (for the moment), I say something like: *How do you feel in your body? What does it feel like to write this way?*

I bring their attention to the feelings they have just experienced — flow, inspiration, being in the zone, whatever you want to call it — so they become conscious of what they felt in their bodies and can come to call upon the memory of this experience as needed.

This is not unlike the moment Gallwey describes of reproducing a peak experience:

> *One day when I was practicing this form of concentration while serving, I began hitting the ball unusually well. I could hear a sharp crack instead of the usual sound at the moment of impact... I resisted the temptation to figure out why, and simply asked my body to do whatever was necessary to reproduce that "crack." I held the sound in my memory, and to my amazement my body reproduced it time and again.*

The idea is to happen upon the flow through play, and then make conscious your experience of being in the flow, until the day comes when you can reliably, through "body memory," tap into the trance-like state pretty much on cue.

When you're in the zone, you almost feel like a channel, like the writing is coming through you.

Writes Gallwey regarding tennis: "Commonly students use language like 'I wasn't there,' 'Something else took over,' 'My racket did this, or did that,' as if it had a will of its own. But the racket wasn't missing, and the great shot was not an accident, even though you didn't plan it. It was you hitting the ball... without the jabbering... without the normal interference of the mind."

Or in the words of the great transcendentalist poet Ralph Waldo Emerson:

> *Standing on the bare ground, — my head bathed by the blithe air, and uplifted into infinite space, — all mean egotism vanishes. I become a transparent eye-ball; I am nothing; I see all; the currents of the Universal Being circulate through me; I am part or particle of God...*

CHAPTER 6

Product and Process

For some reason, when it comes to writing, people get product and process confused. That would be like speaking about the frame of the house (structure) and the wood (words) you use to frame it as if that were a description of how you go about building it. The "what" is not the "how." But no one tells you this. That was part of the reason I suffered so long from writer's block.

Product is what you are aiming for, what it should look like when it's done.

Process is how you get there.

To write a good college essay — or anything, for that matter — you need to know the difference between them.

When it comes to a physical act such as bread-making or painting or building a house, it's easy to distinguish between the *process* it takes to create (the product) and the *product* you have when you're finished.

When your teacher provides you with a rubric for your essay — it must have a thesis, use original sources as evidence, take a stand, be persuasive — these are all elements of product.

When they tell you *how* to structure the essay — put a grabber up front, speak about one of your challenges, end with a bang — this is also product. You can't structure something that doesn't exist!

They tend to say nothing about how you write this essay — how you generate the content that will later be organized into a structure. And they act like it's just a matter of one, two, three. In fact, trying to fit yourself into a structure before you've generated any content is a sure way to encounter writer's block.

In the words of one of my students looking back on his process:

> *I started off in a very mechanical fashion. My first essays were built like brick houses: I would frame the story, tell the story, then make some broad statement in an effort to sound insightful. I used the same language I would use to tell the story in person, long bulky sentences that sort of danced around what I was trying to say without ever saying it. This caused my essays to be extremely removed. Reading those essays was like looking at the event I was describing from 100 feet in the air, with none of those personal and vivid details that I eventually learned to craft my stories with.*

Once you've generated more content than you'll ever need, you can think about how it all might fit together.

Then it's time to play with possibilities. "Play" (again) is the key word here. Writing is most effective if you think of it as play rather than work, and if you do it with an almost reckless abandon.

One question I ask students is to pick out a powerful first line, something that will really grab the reader's attention. For Aaron, it was: "Many players started weeping, some got angry, I simply put my head down."

It's at this point I always say, "There aren't a million possibilities, there are infinite."

The choice you make will be the right one — if it works.

But you could always do it a different way, start somewhere else — however the spirit moves…

You might think that the best way to write a college essay is to look at the prompt and start writing. That makes sense: It is, after all, the shortest distance between two points.

My experience with students, and as a writer myself, however, has shown me that only on a few rare occasions does this actually work.

You sit down, straighten your tie, and start writing. And *voila*, you have an essay you've written from beginning to end. This is a dangerous piece of luck, I like to say, because it leads you to believe you can do this every time.

But writing, like thinking, is not linear. The mind is a wild animal! Trying to rein it in is similar to herding cats. It's nearly impossible.

It's just a shame that no one tells you this in advance. Quite the contrary. They lead you to believe that since a piece of writing must have an introduction, and the introduction is at the beginning, you start by writing the introduction first. You can try it, but it's pretty hard to introduce a topic before you know what you want to say. The mind is more round about than that.

Though you won't often find writing teachers making the distinction between product and process, that's not to say you shouldn't try to get help from all sources. If you notice your eyes glazing over or your stomach knotting up when you're listening to someone's advice, however, move on. You don't want to expose yourself to anything that will make you nervous. Rather, anything you can do to remain calm, anything that will help you achieve "relaxed concentration," is a good thing.

There's no harm in looking at the prompts for the Common App. You may get ideas just from reading them. I often read them aloud to students and ask them if anything comes up for them.

But remember, they are just prompts. They are meant to trigger ideas. In fact, prompt 7 is "Topic of Your Choice." In reality, you can write on anything you want.

There's no harm doing anything that generates ideas.

If reading "Stopping by Woods on a Snowy Evening" makes you think of the winter your grandfather died and you ran out into the snow and wouldn't come back home, then Robert Frost's famous little poem served as a prompt for you.

Or perhaps it was a dream you had... a snippet of conversation... a moment of musing on the hidden benefits of paper clips. One such essay appears in the Breakthrough Essays at the end of this book.

So it really doesn't matter what gets you going. It only matters *that* you get going. And honestly, anything can trigger that.

CHAPTER 7

The Free Write: Hope in the Dark

*You don't start out writing good stuff. You start out writing crap
and thinking it's good stuff, and then gradually you get better at it.*
— Octavia E. Butler

You can always edit a bad page. You can't edit a blank page.
—Jodi Picoult

*Start writing, no matter what. The water does not flow until the
faucet is turned on.* — Louis L'Amour

If I had a writing mantra, a kind of overarching statement or
underlying philosophy that articulates the method to my madness
while working with students, it might be something like: One must
get lost in order to get found.

Perhaps like Thing Two and Thing One, I am a believer in,
even a producer of, chaos!

It's OK if there's a mess.

To start writing a great college essay, you don't need to know
in advance what you want to be when you grow up, and you don't

need to figure out beforehand whether or not you've had any challenges in your life. You don't need to know what your structure will be ahead of time. And as I keep saying, you don't even need a topic.

Imagine that. How can you write without a topic?

Most teachers will tell you that to begin writing, you need a thesis. You will also read this in books. It's very convincing. Even those who may end up reading your essay tell you to start with an outline or introduction.

Here is advice taken from one liberal arts school's admissions website:

Getting started on your essay—what comes first?

- *Follow the practices that have worked for you in writing essays, compositions, and research papers in high school. Once you decide on a topic, you might want to:*
- *Develop an outline*
- *Determine the best format to present your message and start with a creative lead*
- *Prepare a draft using detailed and concrete experiences*
- *Review and edit the draft for grammar, spelling, punctuation, and word usage*
- *Share your draft with others*
- *Rewrite and edit as necessary*

Don't buy it. You can start writing without a thesis/topic. And even if you may have a topic in mind, as you start writing, the topic may change. That's OK. You don't need to be wedded to your first idea. If you write enough, your topic will become clear. Your topic will present itself to you if you let it. The wand will choose the wizard.

Five Significant Moments

My favorite exercise for helping students start to write is the one I did with Aaron — find five "significant moments" in your life in which you went into an experience one person and came out slightly, or more than slightly, changed. But again, any prompt that prompts the free flow of writing is a good one. I could ask you to name five adjectives that describe you, an object that is particularly meaningful to you, a quotation that sums up one of your primary values, or just "What did you have for breakfast?"

Most students find the five significant moments exercise easy. I remind them that their moments can be as quick as a conversation on a plane, an image that sparked a memory, a weekend trip that was eventful, a dream, or a time in which they had a song they couldn't get out of their heads.

Each moment, by definition, contains a time and a place. If you can find a moment, you automatically have located an experience that unfolded over time — you have a narrative. You also have a setting.

What are the words of the song? Where were you? When was this? What happened before and what happened after? And what did the words mean to you?

I ask students to list these moments in bullet points:

- the time I saw Voyager 1 drop its payload
- the first time I saw my father cry
- the moment I realized I could get an A without being nervous first

Bullet points for brainstorming are fine. I wouldn't use them for any other writing activity, however. They condense, rather than expand. If you rely on bullet points in fleshing out your moments, you may find that what you thought was a great idea goes *poof* when you try to develop it.

Once a student has located these moments, the fun really begins.

The next step is the single most important part of the whole process — the free write.

In the free write, it doesn't matter if you know where you're going. You don't need a destination and you don't need a roadmap.

All that matters is that you get into the zone, find the flow, and let the river take you.

You may free write on a topic of your choice, one that you have brainstormed.

You may free write on anything. As long as you write, write, write.

Stream-of-consciousness, no regard for grammar, punctuation and spelling. You don't even need paragraphs. Only requirement — full sentences

Sometimes to help a student get into the zone, as I will later demonstrate, I do an exercise in which we write a crazy short story in turns. I write a sentence; you write a sentence; I write a sentence; you write a sentence.

Since you never know what I'm going to write, you are free to let yourself be in the moment and respond when the time comes.

Another one of my favorite exercises to get students into the "zone" is to have them pick random phrases from a book — it could be any book — and then write using a phrase or concept as the prompt.

I particularly like books about quantum physics or astronomy — they are very rich in metaphor.

*A **black hole** is a place in space where gravity pulls so much that even light cannot get out. The gravity is so strong because matter has been squeezed into a tiny space. This can happen when a star is dying. **Black holes** can be big or small.*

Any number of phrases from this little paragraph can be the source of inspiration.

Take "squeezed into a tiny space." What does that remind you of? A long car ride with your brothers and sisters? Sitting in the back of the bus? Climbing into a cardboard box to hide from your mom?

And how about a feeling you might get, a "space" you might be in, where "gravity pulls so much that even light cannot get out?"

Recently, during a session with my student Audrey, I pulled off my shelf a small book by Rebecca Solnit called *Hope in the Dark.*

The first phrase I saw when I opened the book:

Imagine what else could have sprung from that morning eight years ago.

While Audrey did the exercise, I did it too. Here is what I wrote:

> *To jump ahead eight years from eight years ago lands me right here writing to you. But let me count back. Where was I living? What was I doing? Perhaps that was the year I witnessed a double homicide in Oakland, California. (Sorry to be so grim. It's a true story, but I will save it for my next book.)*

A random phrase from someone else's writing can prompt you to write an amazing essay.

Anything can, if you are open.

Allow yourself to go sentence by sentence into the unknown. It's not only OK to free associate, it's recommended. Even though it may create a mess, you can always clean it up later.

If you're in the flow, keep going. You may not know what you're writing about, but it will eventually become clear. If you're stuck, find another way to go at it or take a break.

I'm a firm believer in what one of my writing mentors used to call "the tyranny of what works."

The flow has power. It indicates that you are onto something. Go with it as long as you can.

Eventually a pattern, a common thread, a purpose will reveal itself.

It will come to make sense just as I came to see that the book I pulled off the shelf wasn't so random after all, as free writing will give you *hope in the dark!*

Students are generally taught very formulaic ways of writing in school. They are made to write five-paragraph, analytical essays following a defined set of criteria.

I'm asking you to unlearn what you know about writing five-paragraph essays, and try a completely different way of going about getting your thoughts down on paper.

In the words of my student Niko:

Transitioning from the style of writing I'd been taught all of high school to the style I needed for college essays was probably the most difficult part of this process. I'd been told for years that I should never put my feelings into an essay, but now my feelings were the integral piece of my essays, and I had to describe them deeply. I first encountered this wall in my Common App essay. At that time, the draft I had seemed fine to me: it laid out all the information in an organized way, like a nice neat package. I didn't know how to slow down and zoom in on crucial moments. I was glossing over them in a few words. I felt lost and frustrated. Every high school teacher of mine would have told me that my essay was great, but here that wasn't good enough.

I suppose you could sum up the free write as *Write first. Think later!*

The idea is to free yourself enough to write whatever comes to mind.

You could write about a teacher you had.

You could write about a drone you tried to build.

You could write about the corner of your backyard that you always believed was haunted.

It doesn't really matter. Anything you write about in great depth, from your heart, in the spirit of freedom, will reveal a lot about you.

So anything can inspire you if you're free to be inspired.

Once you start writing, you may find yourself far afield from your original "triggering subject." That's fine. You've succeeded in allowing the creative part of yourself to have free rein while the critic sits in the corner cleaning its fingernails. At the very least, free writing will help you get the rusty water out of the faucet before it becomes clear.

On this very subject, Richard Hugo, in his book *The Triggering Town*, explains:

> *Your triggering subjects are those that ignite your need for words. When you are honest with your feelings, that triggering town chooses you. Your words used your way will generate meanings. Your obsessions lead to your vocabulary. Your way of writing locates, even creates, your inner life. The relation of you to your language gains power. The relation of you to the triggering subject weakens.*

The time will come for the critic to emerge and see how the whole thing might fit together. You want to put that moment off as long as possible so the imagination can be free to make a mess before the fish pipes up and warns that Mother will soon be home.

CHAPTER 8

Navigating the Deep End

To help you understand something about resistance, about obstacles in the path, let me tell you more about Niko.

Astute, articulate, self-assured, Niko came to me in search of I don't know what. His parents probably told him it was a good idea. I'm not sure he thought so.

The first session, Niko threw down on the table between us drafts he had already written. "I've written the essays already," he said.

My standard response at such times is: "I'm not going to look at these until I give you some tips. That way the student doesn't take it personally if I determine the best course is to start over.

But Niko refused to free write.

That's difficult for me because free writing is the mainstay of my method. It is the "go to" for generating content out of thin air.

Of course, I don't argue with excellence. If someone hands me a brilliant essay, I don't send them back to the drawing board.

For six weeks, Niko wrote draft after wooden draft, hoping it would sprout wings.

Finally, exasperated, he said, "OK, tell me again, what is the free write?"

We tried significant moments first.

"Choose five moments that stand out for you, moments in which you went into an experience one person and came out someone else."

He chose "zorching" down the hill with his friends. (Zorching, apparently, is sliding down on your butt.)

He chose the time he was asked to watch a real-time video in order to get the certificate he needed to become a lifeguard — security camera footage of a kid being thrown by an irresponsible lifeguard into the deep end, flailing, fighting for his life, and eventually drowning.

And his third moment was one in which he saw one of his closest friends — who had been diagnosed as bipolar — "go off the deep-end."

Still believing free writing is an exercise in futility, determined to hold out hope his essays could be done another way, "So?" Niko said. "What are we supposed to do now?

"Do these moments have anything to do with one another?" I asked him.

"No," he said. "I don't see it."

"Deep end?"

His eyes widened.

"Drowning?"

I never had to struggle to get Niko to free write again. In fact, he became my free-writing champion.

Below is Niko's essay (I quoted part of it in the introduction), and following that, his free writes. The free writes combined were about 2,700 words long. In the process of discussing the connections between all three significant moments, Niko came to see that in some way they were all about responsibility —

accepting it in the process of becoming a lifeguard, consciously abandoning it (zorching down the hill) just before having to assume it in earnest, or realizing one isn't (always) responsible for the lives of others. Niko is the oldest of four sons. Perhaps this fact had something to do with his coming back again and again to the topic of responsibility.

In your own writing, you may not make the connections at first. Or you may need to write more until the underlying threads become clear. There may not be enough to go on until you've spit out/written a lot.

This essay got Niko into every school to which he applied. He's currently at UCLA.

I looked around the attic room after the video ended. My fellow lifeguards were crying. A minute ago, the counselor on screen threw a child into the air, then turned his back. The child splashed down into the water. Stroke after stroke, he struggled towards the wall. One last, futile stroke, and he became motionless. The grainy security camera footage showed the lifeguard walking away from her post for a soda. After six infuriating minutes, she finally saw the child and jumped into the pool. Laying his limp body across her arms, she carried him out. My heart dropped into my stomach. She began CPR on the pool deck. But it was too late.

We all just sat there in silence. My boss started saying something to sum the video up, but I wasn't listening. All I could think of was that child, face down in the water. What did I just witness? I felt a cold feeling in my gut and shivered. Real death happens at pools. If someone died on my watch, I'd be the one at fault. Should I talk to my boss and tell her I'm not cut out for this? Suddenly, I saw an image of myself taking action. I pictured myself diving into the pool for an unconscious child. Grabbing his bloated body. His parents watching. Beginning compressions on his cold chest. The look of his unconscious face. What if he doesn't make it? But I wasn't going to quit. Yes, I thought. I'm ready to accept the duty of saving lives.

It was only two summers before that I was zorching down the hillside with my friends, kicking up clouds of dust. Our shouts echoed off the surrounding mountains. After reaching the bottom, climbing through a river, and eventually finding the trail, we hiked triumphantly through camp, down to the showers. "Should we get our shampoo and swimsuits?" someone asked.

"No way!" we decided.

"Let's just shower in our clothes!"

There was no stress there, no deadlines or frustration. We were making silly choices, but they were our choices and no one else's. I felt an intoxicating new independence for the first time. I was right at the cusp of the freedom of high school and the duty that would come with that freedom—in a sweet spot between responsibility and gallivanting. This version of me could never have known the upcoming challenges, but I've grown a lot since then.

Recently, my friend Andrew was in crisis. "My parents took me to a mental hospital. They put me in the Quiet Room. My five-panel hat was with me the whole time," he said. I was with him when he bought that green hat. But my friend Andrew wasn't himself anymore. In fact, he had gone completely off the deep end. I tried to help him find himself again by including him in a gig with my band, but I spent a huge amount of energy trying to keep him organized and happy. It was exhausting. After years of trying to throw him a lifeline, nothing changed. As freshmen we wore his custom t-shirts. At summer camp we listened to his rants. As juniors we gave him feedback on his songs. I eventually realized that it didn't matter how much life force we exerted trying to bring Andrew back. We couldn't make a difference even if we devoted all of our time to him.

Looking back, it seems ironic to me: the summer before I had decided I was responsible enough to save someone's life, but now I felt completely helpless with Andrew. I had to recognize that regardless of how hard I try, there will be aspects of my life that are simply out of my control. It's difficult to face, but what I've learned is this: You can't save everyone from drowning.

Here are Niko's free writes, organized by date. He drew his essay from these. These might give you a better sense of what a free write looks like. Niko's are pretty well-formed. Often free writes are more chaotic. Still, he wrote without knowing where he was headed. I did not edit or proofread his free writes, so what you see is what you get.

May 7, 2016

Last summer when I was working as a lifeguard, at the beginning of the summer they got all of the staff together up in the top room of the Piedmont Rec Center and showed us a video that they told us they really had to show. It was a security camera clip of about 10-15 minutes that showed footage of a little kid drowning due to some extreme neglect by the lifeguards on duty. Some people in the room were very visibly emotional I remember, and it was definitely super disturbing for me, but the most important thing I remember is the thought process I went through in my mind that totally changed my perspective about being a lifeguard and the position I was in. Up until that point, from the time I decided I would take the lifeguard class many months before that, to when I got hired, to my first shift and couple months working watching lap swim in the spring, I had had a little bit of anxiety about being responsible for people's lives. It's a huge duty to have, especially at 16, especially as my first job. But it had seemed really fun, and I felt prepared from the training. I didn't think about it too much because I knew I would've known the steps to go through had there been an emergency on my watch. But after watching this video, I felt like I had to come to terms with the anxiety I was having. The guards in the video were so clearly goofing off and not taking their jobs seriously, with a child dying right in front of them, it was totally frustrating and sad to see this tragedy happen because of some kids not realizing the gravity of their responsibility. I kept thinking about how they would never be able to forget that for the rest of their lives, how without thinking they chose hanging out and getting a soda over saving a kid's life. It seemed so unnecessary that what I realized was probably the exact intended thought process for my bosses at the pool. I acknowledged to myself that I was working at a place where I was in charge of people's lives, which is huge and scary, and that in an emergency I would have to know exactly what to do. That was worrying, since I'd never been in a real life-or-death situation before and didn't know how I might do under pressure. But the next thing I realized is that I'd taken that on, and it was something totally possible for me to do. I could be confident, and know what I'm doing, and be responsible and in charge of people, which actually felt really good and relieving because I just came to the conclusion that I could be a competent lifeguard. That sounds silly... but what I mean is that I didn't have to be anxious. I could change that anxiety into confidence by thinking about how my whole job is to protect against anything like that video happening again. So the community trusted me, and I trusted myself, which was nice to feel. I went into it kind of trying to hide those little ugly thoughts that I may not be totally ready for what I'm taking on, but came out of the experience being confident in myself and realizing that I was going to be able to rise to the occasion and fulfill my responsibility. The other good news is that it was a very safe summer at the pool and I didn't even have to do any rescues, but got experience guarding, teaching lessons, and practicing in staff training.

May 8, 2016

Grainy security camera footage with a date in the bottom of the corner and no audio except for a narrator shows a swimming pool at a summer camp with two lifeguards watching and a bunch of kids in the water. The narrator reads off the names of key figures in the video, a counselor and one specific kid who are both in the pool and the two lifeguards on duty. The kid is about four years old and the counselor and lifeguards are in their late teens. They are circled in red as their full names are read out. The video continues on in real time and narrates as the counselor in the water plays around with some of the kids, tossing them up into the air and letting them splash back down. The kids are loving it, of course, and are all trying to pile on to the counselor so he can toss them again. But a couple minutes into the video, the counselor throws one kid into the air several times in a row, leaving him in deeper water than he began in, and then turns away to handle some of the other kids, assuming that the first one made it back to the wall. This kid, however, does not make it to the wall, and begins floating face down in the water. At this point, or at least within thirty seconds, the lifeguards on duty are legally required to jump into the water and pull the child out, in what would be considered a small to medium sized rescue. But the lifeguards are so preoccupied and negligent that they do not notice the floating kid for almost six minutes. During this time, the video shows the child floating face down in the water, along with silence broken only by the narrator calling out how much time has passed in thirty second increments. It also shows and narrates the lifeguards on duty going to get sodas for themselves, talking to their friends, and walking right up next to the drowning child but somehow not noticing him. Finally, after an infuriating amount of time, one of the guards on duty realizes what's happening, jumps in the pool, and carries the child out of the water, proceeding to attempt CPR. This is far too late, though, as he has already been dead for several minutes. The video cuts off abruptly.

Several seconds after my friend in front of me drops down onto the steep trail, I jump in behind him. Clouds of dust fly as we slide down the hillside, a tiny avalanche of dirt and pebbles following us. I hear the hollering of my best friends and my new friends echoing off the surrounding mountains as they all follow me down the hill. I catch the front of my foot and tumble head-over-heels and come up laughing. Seconds later, I duck and slide under a low-hanging tree branch. I feel like I'm in a movie, tactically and messily tumbling down the side of this hill at camp. Eventually we all reach the bottom of the hill. I look over at my grinning friends, youthful and carefree smiles tainted with a little bit of dirt, just like I'm sure my mouth is. This is so much better than Six Flags. I'm at my first session at the two week long sleepover camp Camp Trinity on the Bar 717 Ranch, up in the Trinity Alps. It's one of the first nights at camp, and what we've just done is called "zorching," a camp tradition of sliding down a homemade trail on one of the neighboring hills around camp. We hike triumphantly back through camp, all the way down to the showers. "Should we get our shampoo and swimsuits?" someone asks. "No way!" we all decide. "Let's just shower in our clothes!" So we all just get in the shower still wearing all our clothes. I'm smiling the whole time. There is no stress here, no deadlines or frustration or complicated relationships that leave people's feelings hurt. We are making silly choices, but they're our choices and no one else's. I can feel my newfound independence, and it's intoxicating. I'm right at the beginning of the freedom of high school, in a sweet spot between responsibility and gallivanting.

Now it's a year later, at the same camp, in the same exact place. My friend Andrew (not his real name) is completely off the deep end, and it makes my stomach hurt. It's nighttime on the platform, and most of us are in our beds. I'm lying in my sleeping bag, trying not to listen too much but still listening to Andrew's wild story as he tells it out to the small group of my friends clustered around his bed. He is describing a night where he got so out of control and angry at his family that he had to be taken to the hospital. He says something about wearing his green five panel hat, a hat that I had bought with him on one of the first days that he started acting like this. I try to turn over and my side and just go to sleep. I still can't stop listening, though. "My parents took me to a f***ing mental hospital in Concord," says Andrew. "They put me in a room called the quiet room and that was where I could just do whatever the f*** I wanted to do." I've never heard this much detail about what was really going on. "It's all my parents' fault," Andrew continues. "They're restricting me. They're not letting me be creative." As Andrew's closest connection to my group of friends, I was let in on some minimal details of what was going on, but the rest of my friends basically knew nothing. A couple feet away from me through the summer night, I hear this heavy information being dropped on all of them, and it hits them hard. "That's so crazy man," someone says. "My five panel was with me the whole time in the hospital," says Andrew. "They gave me medication, but I don't want to take it." All of my friends look confused and scared as they hear about our friend Andrew's descent and see that he's clearly still not okay. Still over on my own bed, I feel sick to my stomach as I think back to the carefree way that we spent our last summer at camp just one year before this, falling and sliding down the hillside with not a worry in our minds. It's such a shame that everything is more complicated now, that that simple and stress-free friendship we all shared last summer has levels to it now. My friend has a mental health issue, and all of us, his friends, have tried without success to help him in any way we can. He clearly can't open up to his parents, and because of their embarrassment they don't want to make it clear to the people in his life that he really needs support in this time. I'm still just a young teenager, and the social complexity is overwhelming, especially when I feel like something needs to be done to help my struggling friend. It's infuriating to not have the knowledge or power to help him. He's right in front of me, intensely sad, intensely lonely, intensely helpless, and I'm exhausted trying to help him return to normal, if "normal" is even possible anymore.

My mind reels as the room is momentarily silent after the end of the video. What did I just witness? This is probably the most disturbing footage I've ever seen. I look around the small attic room and see a lot of my fellow lifeguards crying. My boss is saying something to sum up the video. This is insane. Real death happens at pools, and I'm the one who is responsible if that does happen. I went through all of the training, but that doesn't really mean that I feel prepared to have a child's life in my hands. Is this too much for me? To avoid an incident that haunts me for the rest of my life, I need to know exactly what I'm doing or I need to leave this job. Should I talk to my boss and tell her I'm not cut out for this? No, I can't do that. This is what I've chosen to do and I've already been practicing easy shifts all spring. So I have no other option besides being on top of my game. And that's fine. It's something that's possible for me to do. I can either be tentative and scared every time I'm on stand, or I can be confident in my lifesaving ability and diligently carry out the job I've agreed to do with the knowledge that I'm mentally prepared to have a person's life in my hands. It's not about reading the lifeguard manual fifty times or memorizing exact oxygen percentages. It's about this moment, this transition that I'm having right now. I'm not going to settle for being good enough in this situation, I'm going to be so confident that by the time I actually make a rescue I'll be calm and composed, knowing how many times I've practiced and knowing that I'm ready to save a person's life. This is the moment where I step up to my responsibility, where no parents are here to help me, and it's not necessarily fun, but I'm making this choice on my own. With the option to bail and take a safer job with less responsibility, in this moment I know I want to stay at this job and do it better than anyone else, better than I would have even pictured when I took it. I'm old enough to decide what I want to do, to recognize the heavy implications and know that I'm now strong enough that I can handle them.

I suppose this process is a bit like how Michelangelo describes creating sculptures:

> *Every block of stone has a statue inside it and it is the task of the sculptor to discover it. I saw the angel in the marble and carved until I set him free.*

In some way, the writer has to create the slab he/she will work on/with — and trust there's an angel inside waiting to be discovered and set free.

In this case, the angel might be freedom itself — the free write — which holds the key to its own salvation.

There always is an angel. You have to trust that.

CHAPTER 9

Writing Behind Your Own Back

Maybe I had escaped into some kind of waking dream. Maybe into my animal mind. Yet when I finished filling in the last bit of black, and I leaned back in my desk chair, there it was: the pond, with ripples. I kinda couldn't believe it. It had seemed like I was just making marks, but no, I was making a pond. Behind my own back, as it were. —Clifford Chase

If you have already brainstormed an idea or ideas for your essay, you can begin free writing at any time.

But remember, you can always start writing first and write yourself into a topic kind of by accident or, as Clifford Chase puts it, "behind [your] own back."

As I described in Chapter 2, I eventually came to have ready-access to the trance-like state. And now I am so close to it, I sometimes can't tell if I'm awake or asleep.

To get someone else into that state, that's another story.

I am sure the act or art of doing this is what often makes me feel more like a muse-wizard, an angel of waking dreams, a literary hypnotist.

It's quite a yoga pose I sometimes have to get into to do my job well.

I can't just say, "Forget everything you've learned, let go and trust your intuition!"

I could say it, but in the form of a directive such as this, it might backfire. It might *create* anxiety, not relieve it!

So what do I do instead?

I'm not sure what to answer here. It's different every time.

I guess I trust my own intuition as I am asking you to do. I must invent a pathway that never existed, on the spot, because one is needed.

Sometimes I suggest my fellow traveler hop on my imaginary surfboard and ride the waves with me, to bend and lean in sync with me, to feel it in their bodies. I model what I'm talking about by doing it in front of my students and asking them to follow along.

Sometimes I invent an exercise that will trick them into getting into the zone, such as I recently did with Kai. I took him through an exercise I used to do with a whole class.

I started by writing a cliff-hanging sentence on the top of a blank page of a yellow legal pad. I asked him to continue the story with one sentence of his own. He did. I followed suit. And so on, back and forth, until we got to the end of the page.

At that point I said, "Now you end it with at least one element that was in the first sentence I wrote."

In this game, the curve ball, the unexpected, the element of surprise throws you into a state in which your usual ammo doesn't work. You have to rely on Thing Two and Thing One.

Ironically, I have also used rigid structures as a way to shake things up.

I might ask you to write a paragraph using only one-syllable words or give you restrictions such as "No adjectives allowed," "No being verbs." Even, "Everything in dialogue."

Writing in strict forms such as the *villanelle* or the *sestina* is another way to introduce structure to reduce anxiety.

I am not suggesting that the essay as a whole be written in the form of a villanelle or a sestina, though it could.

Once you escape the prison you don't even know you're in, slip through the cracks of your own anxiety, things open up. The raucous twins have taken over. You're then able to write from "the zone."

When Kai was finished with the story, by the way, he was so pleased with himself, he asked to write another.

In fact, I was originally hired to work with Kai on preparing him for the SSAT's because he was suffering from such intense test anxiety he could never perform to the level of his ability. Even speaking about the test made him nauseous.

Enter "Crazy One-Line Fiction!"

"That's so amazing!" I said when I read his final line.

Kai flashed me a shy smile.

"See if you can feel what you're feeling. Pause for a moment and feel it in your body. You can even close your eyes to get a better feel."

Kai closed his eyes for about six seconds.

He was calm and happy, he told me.

"That feeling. You can return to it at any time. You can remember this moment — the sun cutting a yellow line on the wall across from our table, me sitting here looking at you, the funny last line you invented. When you get nervous or upset, or just lose your bearings, return to this moment, return to the feeling inside."

As another student describes it: "I know I can trust myself and the decisions I need to make by what I feel inside. If I feel like I'm on top of that hill watching the sunset, happy and free, I know that's the right path to follow."

I have also often used music as a muse. Sometimes if a student is really stuck, I will have him or her write to music. Sometimes I pick the song, sometimes they do.

Recently I worked with a student trying to get into RISD and Pratt who was very smart and very creative — visually. When it came to writing, he froze.

Finally, after many failed attempts to get him to let go, I asked him what made him feel the most happy. He told me it was this song he loved by Frank Ocean. We listened to it together. Then he wrote, in one sitting, the paragraph below. That paragraph flowed so easily and was so clear and beautiful, I knew it was important.

"Moon River" walks a thin line between order and chaos. Ocean sings, seeming sad and wistful, his tone mirroring the longing lyrics. His layered vocals finish one line with two words, unsure. I can relate to his lack of conviction, his second-guessing. The guitar that has played only backup to his singing swells and floods the song with a strong confidence. The layers of his voice fill many levels and guitars in each ear nearly overpower the song, until the guitars masterfully devolve into spacey synths and sounds that seem to be always in motion. I find myself understanding the journey of the song as it relates to my own, moving from uncertainty to assurance. The remaining instrumentals lose their clashing individuality and become one melody. Though the confidence has peaked and uncertainty begins to return, it's not with the same confusion as the beginning. There is a sort of acceptance in his voice that I recognize

in my own life. Though jumbled and offbeat, the song never returns
to quite the level of lostness with which it begins.

"What do you like about this song?" I asked Alex.

"How the melody gets lost and then resolves itself," he said.

"Has that ever happened to you?"

He began to list moments in his life in which he was terrified, shied away, lost confidence, and how he pushed through these moments to a stronger and more assured sense of self.

He free wrote the scenes that begin the essay — his first experience with ice hockey and his terror of speaking in front of the class. All he had left to do was create transitions and write a conclusion to tie it all together.

Here's Alex's essay:

I took the stairs from the locker room to the ice one at a time, feeling like I weighed twice as much as normal, teetering on two blades, each only a half inch thick. I was told the classes were skill-based, but I had been put in a group with the elementary school kids. Humiliated, I decided hockey was not for me. "What's the worst that could happen?" my parents pleaded. So I committed myself to at least try. It was a short class and I didn't know anyone there. *Who cares if I mess up?* On the ice, I panicked as the knives on my feet slid out of my control. Now, three years later, I am a starting forward on the team.

It was one thing to bumble around the ice and another to get up on stage. I was so shy I couldn't even tell my new drama teacher how shy I was. "Everyone else is going up. You could try at the end?" she proposed. I agreed, having absolutely no intention of going at all. I sat and watched my new classmates walk up to introduce themselves, one at a time. I admired the ones who spoke with ease, like they had been doing this all their lives. They were kids, just like me, but they somehow felt more self-assured. Others reminded me of myself: nervous, shaky, and quiet. But unlike me, they didn't ask our teacher to go last. These kids were showing me up on the first day, and in that moment, there was no better motivator than the shame of being the only one who chose to go unnoticed. I prepared myself as the alphabet neared its close. My turn. Taking a deep breath, I shuffled to the front of the small crowd. I stammered out my name, immediately regretting my decision. I looked over at my teacher expecting to see disappointment, but she looked so encouraging, smiling and nodding as if to say, "Keep going." All I did was say my name, and it was enough of a triumph to eventually land me a role in the school play.

Whenever I think back to that cold morning in drama class or that even colder ice rink, it makes me think of Frank Ocean's cover of "Moon River," in which his slow and layered voice conveys complex emotions, one moment unsure and questioning, the next confident and full.

"Moon River" walks a thin line between order and chaos. Ocean sings, seeming sad and wistful, his tone mirroring the longing lyrics. His layered vocals finish one line with two words, unsure. I can relate to his lack of conviction, his second-guessing. The guitar that has played only backup to his singing swells and floods the song with a strong confidence. The layers of his voice fill many levels and guitars in each ear nearly overpower the song, until the guitars masterfully devolve into spacey synths and sounds that seem to be always in motion. I find myself understanding the journey of the song as it relates to my own, moving from uncertainty to assurance. The remaining instrumentals lose their clashing individuality and become one melody. Though the confidence has peaked and uncertainty begins to return, it's not with the same confusion as the beginning. There is a sort of acceptance in his voice that I recognize in my own life. Though jumbled and offbeat, the song never returns to quite the level of lostness with which it begins.

I've always struggled to find my moments of assurance, my very own layering, where everything that was disjointed and uncertain shifts into unity, even just for a second. I still sometimes struggle with a moment of shakiness, but I've found that I can always count on myself to grow steady and bring in a new, however temporary, harmony of confidence.

If, like Alex, you can push through your moments of "shakiness" in the writing process, you too may find that "everything that is disjointed or uncertain shifts into unity."

CHAPTER 10

The Power of Association

A writer writes, and if he begins by remembering a tree in the backyard, that is solely to permit him gradually to reach the piano in the parlor upon which rests the photograph of the kid brother killed in the war. —William Saroyan, *Starting with a Tree and Finally Getting to the Death of a Brother.*

In this mode of not-knowing, the thick-torsoed, literal, and crew-cut conscious mind is moved to the sidelines in favor of the swinging, perceptive, light-footed, tutu-wearing subconscious.
—George Saunders

Once a year, every year at The Saint Ann's School for Gifted and Talented in Brooklyn, New York, where I taught for many years, the English Department runs a "writing marathon." This is a week-long event in which every day students are given a new, often wacky assignment: Write a poem about the letter P, Q, or R, pretend you are a [pick the kind of bird], write a poem in which the first letter of each word spells your name…

The sheer volume of assignments, that they keep coming at you from left field, so that it doesn't matter whether what you write is "good" or not — there are just too many assignments to care — this is what made the Writing Marathon so successful. Some of my students, the novelist Ivy Pochoda for one, went on to become famous writers. Robert Levy, another. They never told me so, but I bet they would say that the Writing Marathon set them free and perhaps even marked the beginning of their literary careers.

I always did the assignments side by side with my students. While they were writing, I was writing too. In fact, from one prompt I wrote a whole book of poems, *La Capra*.

This book originated from a Writing Marathon exercise of "imaginary translation." We were given a poem in Polish — I still remember the title: *"Desitva Oblast"* — to translate into English.

My students wrote these hilarious poems about blasting destiny or the new rock sensation "Desitva."

Later, I found a poem in Italian called *La Capra* and "translated" it fifty-five times. Here is the poem in Italian. Following is one of my "translations."

La Capra
Ho parlato a una capra.
Era sola sul prato, era legata.
Sazia d'erba, bagnata
dalla pioggia, belava.
Quell'uguale belato era fraterno
al mio dolore. Ed io risposi, prima
per celia, poi perche il dolore e eterno,
ha una voce e non varia.
Questa voce sentiva
gemere in una capra solitaria.

In una carpra dal viso semita
sentiva querelarsi ogni altro male,
ogni altra vita.

— *Umberto Saba*
da Casa e campagna, 1909-1910

The Goat
Hey ho, I'm talkin' to a goat.
Hanging loose in the sun, high on life
He's chompin' on the grass.
I'm just piddling around, who cares.
I have an ugly beast of a brother.
All the worse for me. His name is Eddie Risposi,
first born, he pains me eternally. He has a disgusting
monotone voice, blek.
What a sensitive voice this solitary goat has.
I like talkin' to this goat.
No quarrels, he just eats grass.
No problem.

I include the poem and one of its translations here to illustrate how nonsensical, unconscious, and seemingly random associations can be. Sometimes it was the look of a word that led me to a phrase or idea, sometimes the sound. Since I don't know Italian, all I could do was free associate.

The mind naturally moves from one idea to the next, from branch to branch, like a nimble chimpanzee. As soon as you start trying to figure out a structure, worry about the order of ideas, allow the critic to take over — the blood supply to your associations will be cut off.

Take your associations seriously, even if they seem random, wacky, out of left field. There is often a hidden sense to them which will eventually be revealed. Sometimes, in the moment, you have to trust the unknown and just let yourself go with it. When this happens to me, I often feel almost giddy, like I'm flying. Here is Clifford Chase's beautiful description of this kind of moment:

> *When I'm writing well, I feel like I'm crawling further and further out on a limb, and the limb can't hold my weight much longer. This isn't a light-footed sensation, but I'm kind of laughing while I'm doing it, drunk on my own audacity. Am I wearing a tutu? If so, I'm a chimp in a tutu, a circus animal on the loose, and when the limb is just about to break, yes, I swing to the next one.*

A seemingly random prompt can be the inspiration for a whole book.

You never have to worry that you got the idea from someone or something else.

Everything you do, and everything you write, is generated from your own psyche. Your thoughts and sentences will have echoes and connections you don't even know are there. That's part of the fun — unearthing them like hidden treasures out of the flotsam and jetsam of what Mary Oliver describes as your "wild and precious" mind. What you write will be yours no matter what, so take inspiration wherever you can find it.

All you need is to be willing to venture into uncharted territory. You must be open to getting lost in order to get found.

CHAPTER 11

The Yoga of Writing

*We call upon the waters that rim the earth, horizon to horizon,
that flow in our rivers and streams, that fall upon our gardens and
fields, and we ask that they teach us and show us the way.*
— Chinook Blessing Litany

I have found that one of the easiest ways to get into the
"trance-like state" is through the body.

That can seem difficult when you are sitting in one position for
hours looking at your computer screen or hunched over a blank
piece of paper.

If the words are flowing, as I've said, go with the flow.

If you just can't get anything going, it might help to move
around. Sometimes just a quick breath of fresh air will help. Take
a walk. Shoot some hoops. Swim. Dance. Take a nap. Come back
to it later. I often have my best ideas in the shower.

You can also take a brief break and try doing some yoga.

In the course of writing this book, I ran some of the basic
premises of my method by my girlfriend who is a yoga teacher.
She was intrigued and asked me questions about how I got

students to tap into the deeper parts of themselves, how I got them to bypass "the thinking mind."

"Bypassing the thinking mind is what yoga is all about," she told me.

There were times in my life when I was really into yoga, but until I met Cheryl, I had never thought to apply yoga to writing.

Recently on a trip to the Yuba River in Nevada City, from the safe haven of our beach towels, lying in the hot sun, side by side, Cheryl and I began to make the connections between her river and mine, and how we navigate our particular rivers — how we sink or swim. And what we saw is that the ways in which she shares the principles and practices of yoga and the ways in which I teach writing have a lot in common.

Our conversation inspired me, and I began to ask her questions. Her answers provide the backbone to a series of yoga poses that will help even the most "stuck" writer open the channels and find the currents to take them down the river.

Is there a first pose you can give me, that will help my writers set an intention and invite in the muse?
Follow this format

Sukhasina/Easy Pose. This pose invites stillness into the body. Grounded seat, open palms, resting gently on the thighs, relaxed shoulders, deep breath connecting to the earth. Inhale into heart center (hands in prayer over breast), hold the intention with a soft open heart.

Once they feel ready to embark, what can they do to trust the process, lift their legs, and let go of fear?

Moving from mountain pose with both feet connected to the earth to balanced tree pose, balancing on one leg pushing down through the standing leg. Arms lift from heart center to the sky. I always think of the body as a conduit connecting heaven and earth. You're connecting down and you're reaching up. Energy flows. Steady and soft, this will allow the energy to flow through you.

Is there a way to help my writers feel safe enough and yet free enough to allow the deeper forces in themselves to find voice?

Holding a standing posture such as Warrior 2 — one foot resting on the other calf — invites strength, stability and power. You're building strength in the legs, drawing upwards. Palms up inviting the "strong" forces to come through you while being grounded, stable and steady through the legs. From there, go to Triangle Pose. You extend in all different directions while drawing energy inward and calling in the spirits, whatever they may be.

My writers may require endurance, stamina, stick-with-it-ness? What can I give them to help them "hold the pose?"

Any time there's strain, pain or loss of balance, come back to the breath. An inhale with equal length as the exhale takes the effort out and brings you back to center… long steady inhale, smooth steady exhale.

And finally, what can I tell them so that they can call upon the "state" that your instruction has given them so they can find the river, or a river, and take it where it goes?

For this I would have them return to and focus on the breath.

Anjali Mudra — Prayer position. Soften heart space. Bow with gratitude that there's a force greater than yourself, like the current of the river, that will take you where you need to go and protect you on the journey.

Jhana Mudra — Thumb and forefinger connects individual self with universal self.

And finally, Om — the universal vibration. Connecting our vibration to life. Creates a vibration where breath and sound meet…

"Perfect," I say to her. "Just as writing expresses the meeting of thought and voice."

From this place of calm power, relaxed concentration, the imagination is free.

As we discussed, sometimes just remembering the feeling is enough to get you started. Yoga can help you remember the feeling.

"You can't feel constricted at the beginning or else the ideas don't flow," my student Mira explains. "You have to let yourself be free. The first time, there might be nothing there. Maybe the second time, too. But if you keep writing, somewhere, hidden in there, will be that one paragraph, that one sentence, that one phrase that will suddenly make you say, 'Yes! This is it!' That is the most gratifying feeling."

CHAPTER 12

The Four Modes of Writing

Don't tell me the moon is shining; show me the glint of light on broken glass. — Anton Chekhov

Once a student has written a free write, I introduce the Four Modes of Writing: Showing, Telling, Analyzing and Reflecting.

Your essays for school are almost always analysis — What were the causes of the Civil War? How did the author create a sense of suspense in this passage?

But now you are tasked with writing a story-essay which must be vivid and engage the reader's body (senses) as well as his or her mind. It's very helpful at this point to have someone who you trust ask you questions and point out where you could be more specific or make the writing more vivid.

Most students write their free writes in "tell." There's nothing wrong with this as a first step. But "tell" can be very dull and create distance between you and the reader.

Here is an example of telling with a bit of reflection: "I had a great time at camp. I met this kid named Josh. We sat by the campfire until the sun went down. I felt very happy. Now we're best friends."

"I felt very happy," is a reflection. Reflection encompasses thoughts, feelings and ideas.

Showing is the crown jewel of the expanded free write. It is your opportunity to bring the reader into the moment with you, to bring to life what you are trying to describe.

Showing has three elements:

- Action
- Dialogue
- Description

Let me demonstrate this by using the same story I just wrote, but this time putting it all in "show" rather than "tell."

"Get that chair over there," Josh said. [Dialogue]

"Which one?" I said. [Dialogue]

"That one," he said. [Dialogue]

He pointed. [Action]

Just at that moment I could see, out of the corner of my eye, a group of gnats having a party in the last rays of sunlight. [Description. Here I don't need to tell the reader it's twilight and I feel happy. "Last rays of sunlight" and "gnats having a party" *show* the reader, through an image, what time of day it is, and how I feel about what's happening.]

Showing will bring the reader closer and infuse life into the story you're trying to tell.

Often your teachers will tell you you should show *instead* of tell. I rather think it's a balance of show and tell with some reflection sprinkled in.

But again, there's not one right way to do it. You could write a wonderful, deep, convincing essay all written in reflection. You have to follow what feels right for you.

In addition to livening it up with "show," you may also have to bring in the "W's" — Who, What, Where, When and Why. When you free associate — jump from one branch to the other — it's easy to leave out details that are clear to you, but may not be clear to your reader. The "expanded free write" is the time to include what you may have left out.

It is also the time to liven up the language.

Once you've free written and done an expanded free write, you're ready to think about structure.

Here is an example of my student Julia's free write with my questions and comments (as her trusted reader) sprinkled throughout. In this case, Julia came up with a topic first — how she struggles to integrate in herself her Brazilian and American identities. Because the writing was vague in places, I sent her back to locate moments that would illustrate what she was trying to express. I also asked her to *show* what she was telling by using dialogue and adding specific details. My comments are bolded. Again, I did not line edit or proofread the free write — that would defeat the purpose. Rather, I ignore issues of spelling, punctuation, capitalization in favor of an holistic view.

Julia asked me to make specific suggestions about where she could add dialogue to this free write:

. . . my culture has always been something i have struggled with. I am the child of immigrants, a first-generation American in an extensive line of Brazilians. **Perfect place to put in stories. Simulate what was told to you. "I never thought I'd come to America," my mom said one day when we were driving to school. Etc etc (of course I'm making it up, but this is the kind of thing you need** → I have grown up hearing the stories of how hard my parents worked to become Americans, to communicate in broken English, and to conform to the cultural customs of a brand new world. When my parents immigrated to America in search of better work, they fought hard for the life they wanted to create. **See if you can ask them or recall moments of this** → They faced racism for their ethnicities, worked for hours on end, and lived with the distance of over 6,000 miles separating them from their families. My father experienced discrimination in his job for being Latino. My mother worked for little money for hours on end and still had the strength to go to school. **This must have been either witnessed or in dialogue. So remember you've got to SHOW as well as tell. That means description, dialogue and action. Pick specific moments and develop these — the time your mom told you such and such, the time you witnessed your dad coming home late, the story he told about being discriminated against...**They didn't even have enough money to make phone calls to Brazil.

A struggle I have encountered with erasure is strong. **What makes you say that? Is it never mentioned? How do you experience this?** → the erasure of cultures I identify with. All my family is Brazilian, but I was born, and have always lived, in America. So what does that make me? It is challenging trying to figure out how much of my identity pertains to either culture. Cultural erasure seems like an easy solution: wipe away one part of my cultural identity, so that **Here would be a place to show how you have done this** → I can more closely conform to another. but cultural erasure is so dangerous. **These are broad concepts. What you need (again) is moments in which these concepts are exhibited or played out. Otherwise, there's nothing to show the reader about what you've experienced.**

Here is the next iteration of Julia's free write:

I am ten. My dress is red and I am wearing the… .I remember being in elementary school and feeling the worst shame whenever **Great specifics in highlighted area** → i would open my lunch box and the smell of the empanada would evoke an "ewww what is that!" from my friends around me. I remember hating the way my eyes were so dark and brown, unlike the blues and greens of my peers. i remember feeling embarrassed whenever my mother would speak to me in Portuguese around my friends. I remember loathing the way my body looked because it wasn't shaped the way the bodies around me were. eventually, this became my world. i pushed away the part of me that made me who i am. I wanted to be what i thought was a "traditional" American and nothing else. when i was younger. **This would be great to break down into "showable" moments. Do you remember these trips? Can you describe one or two? Give us a vivid pictu**re. → my family would take trips down to Brazil to see our relatives almost yearly, but once the housing crisis hit us, we couldn't. so for years, i missed a part of me that had created so much of my identity. **Yay!! This is vivid!!!** → I began to forget about the large plates of steaming beans and rice, the heat of the sand covering little pesky crabs, and loud laughter over drinks at the earliest hours. a year ago, my family took a trip back to Brazil for the first time in seven years.

This is great and a very telling moment!! → I remember when my mom told me that she had bought our tickets. It was just a casual day, and I had just come home from school. I felt the strangest sort of excitement. I felt ecstatic that I was soon going to revisit all my memories that had faded, but at the same time i was nervous about being an American in Brazil. what if I couldn't remember how to say something to my cousins? what if they didn't see me the same way? What if i had become exactly what younger self had wanted? When we arrived there, all my worries faded away. My relatives greeted me with kindness I have never encountered before in my life. this trip, i would say, changed the way i saw myself. **This could be made much more vivid. I have an essay I want to show you or read to you so you can see what's possible to do with this** → of course, i got to see all the aunts and uncles and cousins i had missed for so long, and the beaches i had played on as a child, and the trees that I swung from. but i also got to see Brazil in a way I had never seen it before. I noticed things that I had never noticed before, probably because I was too young to pick up on them. I noticed how the bodies of the women walking down the streets looked like my body. I had the same hair, the same eyes, the same shape as the girls that passed by. I noticed how the foods I ate took me back to a place that I didn't know I remembered. **Super great!** → The soft acarajé, the sweet cocadas, the warm bolinhos de peixe all revived memories of my childhood, of grabbing a treat from a plate on the counter and running off with my friends into the sandy grass. **Is there a way to show this somehow?** I noticed how the love that I was given in Brazil was so much deeper than any love I had encountered in America. Part of me felt like I really belonged. And another part of me felt like a foreigner. My parents laughed at me when I mispronounced a Portuguese word. My aunts and uncles scoffed at me when I acted too "Americana". **Here's a great place for dialogue. Put it in Portuguese.** → My grandmother told me that I sound too much like an American when I speak Portuguese. i wasn't sure where I really belonged. That's devastating and contradicts the fact that you felt loved like nowhere else?

for so long I struggled with figuring out whether I was American or Brazilian, and which parts of me belonged where. But being in Brazil a year ago made me realize that I am not one or the other. I am Brazilian-American. I feel pride in having the ability to say that I feel a connection to America and Brazil alike. I like being able to tell my American friends about customs and foods that are foreign to them, and I like being able to tell my Brazilian family about the great adventures I experience in America. Although I still have certain insecurities of not being like most of my peers, I have learned to embrace the way I look. I feel great honor in being bilingual, and being able to learn more with the language-learning skills I have. I no longer feel shame for the foods that my family enjoys. I cannot dissect my identity into parts that I can categorize as either culture. instead I identify with the culture of being both. I identify with the culture of missing some parts of being Brazilian, and missing some parts of being American. I identify with the culture that seems imperfect to some, maybe most. i am not one or the other, i am not too brazilian to be american or too american to be brazilian. I am proudly Brazilian-American, my imperfections perfectly categorized.

As you can see, Julia alludes to the discrimination her father felt, her own shame and embarrassment, but can do more to show how and when these occurred by picking moments and developing them. Where she tells, the reader gets a sense of what she's feeling or describing. Where she shows, the reader can *feel, taste, see, touch what she's feeling* and is brought into the moment.

There may be quite a few back and forths with your trusted reader before you expand your free write enough so that it is ready to be organized. It's always difficult when your reader finds "fault" or wants more or less of something. Try to resist the temptation to defend yourself. It does no good to tell the reader what you *meant* since you won't be present to explain yourself when the Ad Com reads your essay. If something your reader suggests doesn't feel useful, let it go. Otherwise, welcome whatever advice might be helpful. You kinda have to be a Buddha when it comes to getting feedback.

CHAPTER 13

Order out of Chaos

Oh! Blessed rage for order...
The maker's rage to order words of the sea,
Words of the fragrant portals, dimly-starred,
And of ourselves and of our origins,
In ghostlier demarcations, keener sounds.
—Wallace Stevens, *The Idea of Order at Key West*

You have written a full and thorough free write. You've developed it as much as you can (for the moment). Now it's time to identify and label common threads or related ideas and group them into "clumps." Sometimes they fall into the same categories you started out with before free writing. Sometimes new "clumps" or threads have developed. In a certain way, every essay is a kind of collage. Even if you don't end up using several of your significant moments in one essay — even if you write on one topic and stick with it, such as you will see in the essay on the benefits of paperclips — you will still be piecing together moments related to that topic.

Don't worry, by the way, if you have much more material than you need. You can always trim the fat. Cutting is much easier than generating.

Now is a good moment to pick a first line. From there, you can try putting your clumps in order and write a rough outline. It can be very rough, like Niko's:

1. video of seeing kid drown
2. zorching down the hill
3. my friend Andrew going off the deep end

Then, as if you are making a quilt, create transitions between the sections to stitch the pieces together.

At this point, you have a rough draft.

Sometimes, though rarely, the draft is almost perfect and only needs to be proofread before it is ready to send.

More often than not, however, it contains potholes, glitches, inconsistencies, which you may find difficult to spot with your own eyes. Once again, a trusted reader is invaluable. My own trusted reader helped me see, in this very chapter, places where I needed to re-order my paragraphs. They looked fine to me, but once he pointed that out, I could see where a reader might get lost.

There is Always Pain in Writing

When your story is ready for rewrite, cut it to the bone. Get rid of every ounce of excess fat. This is going to hurt; revising a story down to the bare essentials is always a little like murdering children, but it must be done. — Stephen King

When you read what you've written from start to finish to see whether or not it flows, which I call "the sweep through" — you may experience the pain that seems always to come at some point in the writing process. The pain is not always from letting go of your "little darlings" — those phrases or sections that you may love but which need to be cut — there's also the pain that comes with making sure you're getting it right.

You must ask yourself: Does it make sense? Is it working? Is there anything left out? Am I saying what I want to say? Does one idea flow into the next?

In a certain way, when you arrive at this moment, you have to call in another part of your brain, a different faculty — the editor — to do the work of organization and quality control. At the same time, you cannot put Thing Two and Thing One entirely back in their box. You still need them to generate transitions — possibly even new ideas — that are just as creative and beautifully-expressed as the ones you happened upon in your free write.

I have never been able to put my finger on why there's always this moment of pain in writing.

Is it because the creative and critical are suddenly brought into such close proximity?

Or is it, as King says, because you have to get rid of words, phrases, even whole paragraphs that you loved but can't use in this particular essay?

Perhaps a combination of the two.

In any case, making it all fit together from first word to last, editing and revising until it is as good as it can be, giving it to a trusted reader to help you identify your blind spots — these will make you break a sweat.

But perhaps if you know that ahead of time, it won't scare you quite so much. Stay with the pain. You will get there, and it will pass.

You must hold yourself to a high standard at this point in the process. Each word must do work. You must not gloss over what you've written because you're tired, which you may be. If it is too close to you and you no longer have perspective, put it away for a while (another reason to start early), take a break and come back to it with fresh eyes.

It's sometimes good once you have a draft to read it aloud. If you find your attention flagging, you can be sure that your reader — who is already expecting to be bored — will be nodding off.

You must sweep through and sweep through your essay until you are sure it will do what it needs to — engage the reader enough so that he or she will read from first word to last. If you can succeed in doing this, you'll have a better chance of getting into your school of choice.

I can tell you from my time working in admissions that when I read an essay from start to finish, and was moved to laughter or tears, it was very hard to say "no."

I would look over the rim of my reading glasses at the grades, test scores, recommendations of that particular student, and unless there were red flags, that student got in.

You want to be the student who gives the Ad Com what they don't expect — an authentic, beautifully-expressed essay they can't put down.

CHAPTER 14

The Gift of Stuck-ness

Mira came to me with an unusual amount of depth, openness and natural talent. Nonetheless, she, too, had been trained in the school of five-paragraph essays:

In school, I was taught to go about my writing in a very formulaic way —
structured introduction with a thesis, three body paragraphs with topic
sentences relating to my thesis, and a conclusion. After writing countless essays,
I really did "master" this type of writing. Once I understood the structure, I
was able to embellish it with stronger word choices and smoother flow.

In school, I never really wrote about myself. It was always about book
characters, historical figures, analyzing this and that. But rarely did I use the
"I" voice in writing. Then, this past year I started writing in a journal, just
for fun. I was really surprised when I opened the first page of my notebook
that I had trouble spilling everything out. I can write a five-paragraph essay
but I can't write a simple journal entry?! I think it's a different, yet equally
important, skill to be able to write freely about your own experiences.

With an uncanny wisdom, Mira's Common App essay addresses the topic of "stuck-ness" head on. Mira must have written forty drafts of this essay. The amount of self-reflection it required — to understand why she was shut-down and couldn't hear what a boy from Gaza was saying or feel the "holiness" of the Wailing Wall — and then to identify her own moment(s) of breakthrough — was painstaking. She had to dig deep, to ask herself hard questions, to hold herself to a high standard in terms of whether or not she was articulating exactly what she wanted and was being honest with herself in the process. What amazes me about this essay is that in the end, she finds salvation in the stuckness itself. She finds, as a Zen proverb expresses, that "the obstacle is the path."

In fact, "The obstacle is the path" could be the subtitle of UNSTUCK. It is a great way to frame the difficulties, the blocks, the pain — in writing, as in life.

Here is Mira's essay:

A boy from Gaza sits directly across from me. He speaks angrily of revenge — his hands moving wildly, his voice harsh and pained. I'm thinking: *Audi alteram partem* — "Listen to the other side." This was, after all, the goal of our "dialogue hut."

The first couple of days, I found myself stuck: When someone made a provocative comment, I would either withdraw deeply into myself and be consumed by silence or speak out too soon, adding myself to the noise. These responses brought momentary solace from my own discomfort, but the conflict — within me and within the room — would reemerge, often more intense than it had before. These moment at Seeds of Peace challenged me to my core.

During one rainy day, the boy from Gaza took his wildly moving hands and wrapped them around my throat. "I am weak," he whispered in a pained voice, "Do you hear me?" But I heard nothing. The sound of his voice was overwhelmed by the beat of my heart. I sat unable to respond. Fear had become my place of being. I was numb, paralyzed, silent.

In that moment, he was unreadable to me, as I was to myself, like a holy text written in a foreign tongue. The glimmer in his eyes was lonely, yet his grip was angry. I was confounded and scared.

This feeling was not unfamiliar. On the last day of my Bronfman Fellowship, I stood in front of the Western wall in Jerusalem. All I was thinking about was that pigeon I saw fluttering against the ancient stone. Where I should have been feeling holiness, all I could feel was, well, nothing.

Just then, in the shimmering waves of heat that came off the stone, I remembered myself in the dialogue hut, suddenly woken from a long sleep. I had surprised myself: Standing at the crossroads, I chose to listen intently. I observed, accepted the words I was hearing — not as wrong or right — but simply just as they were.

With listening came understanding. The next day, the same boy, among boys like him, was bowed down in prayer. I stood at the door and heard the focused songs of the worshippers. Even though they sang in a language I didn't understand, I felt like I could hear them. What had changed? I heard the voice inside me say, "Listen, you're not listening." And then I could hear the *kol demamah dakah*, the "still, small voice" within him. I found that "low door in the wall, which others had found before me, which opened on an enclosed and enchanted garden," as Charles describes in *Brideshead Revisited*.

The truth is: the door was inside me, and it opened up to me a new understanding of the Western wall itself. I came to see the wall, and the stuckness of my experience, as a manifestation of holiness — the invisible had become visible. The literal translation of Israel is "to struggle with God." There is something sacred about the "push and pull," the cycle of experiencing clarity and then watching it evaporate.

The entire plan of the universe is filled with roadblocks: Writer's block, a challenging relationship, an impossible math problem, a mid-life crisis, too many choices, not enough choices: these are life's most challenging trials and tribulations. If it hasn't hit you yet, it is bound to at one point or another.

And when it does it feels like two hands wrapped around your neck. You want to cry out, "I am weak. Can you hear me?"

I hope that when I am stuck, as I inevitably will be, I will be graced with the insight that there is something greater than myself — beyond my ability to comprehend. And that even a seemingly unreadable text can lead to what some may call G-d, not only in spite of its difficulty, but because of it.

Mira alludes here to the idea that the stuckness is itself the gift, even though, as we all know, it doesn't feel that way at the moment we are experiencing it. But perhaps, as Zornberg writes, "Every person has a specific form of obscurity, or resistance, that s(he) is challenged to confront in the world. Eternal life, one's personal world, is created by the way in which one struggles to engage with this blind spot."

Mira describes her experience of breakthrough:

I think the biggest breakthrough I had was the power of the free write. This was a life changer. At first it felt incredibly daunting to open up a document and just flush out my ideas — no structure, and most importantly, no deleting anything. Gabby taught me to trust the free write and give myself the freedom to get it all out there. Many times I would panic and say to Gabby, "How is this going to fit in a 200 word essay?!" And every single time, she would tell me to NEVER think about the word count, because you can always cut it down and choose the best parts. I can't feel constricted at the beginning or else the ideas can flow. The first time, there might be nothing there. Maybe the second time too. But if you keep writing, somewhere, hidden in there will be that one paragraph, that one sentence, that one phrase that will suddenly make you say "Yes! This is it!" That is the most gratifying feeling.

CHAPTER 15

Coloring in the Details

Perhaps the second week after I started working with Jonathan, his mother texted me to say he had to cancel our session — his friend was in the hospital and it wasn't looking good.

When I met him a week later, one of his closest friends, Lucas, had died. It was a suicide. Apparently, Lucas had overdosed on Tylenol, fallen into a coma and finally did not make it.

Having only met Jonathan once before, I was at a loss as to how to proceed. Working on college essays seemed almost trivial.

We were speaking on Skype and Jonathan looked at me sadly through the filmy layers the computer screen put up between us.

"I would say we should continue work on the essays, if you're up for it," I said at last.

"I'm up for it," Jonathan said.

Two weeks previous, Jonathan had made a list of his significant moments. He found the task easy. Here's what he wrote:

- The paper chain I made with my friends in fourth grade to try to beat the world's record
- Getting the idea to start my babysitting business

- Winning the public speaking competition
- The day I found out I did not make the soccer team
- When my grandfather gave me his pocket knife

"You think you can write on one of these?" I asked him. "They're really good moments."

"I think so," he said.

He chose first the story about the pocket knife.

After a quick review of what a free write is, a short talk on the four modes of writing, three or four false starts and an attempt to switch topics, still he was blocked.

"I can't write today," he said.

I studied his face.

"Are you sad?"

He nodded.

"Mmmm."

There was a long pause. I sighed. I didn't want to press him. I wasn't sure what to do.

"Could you write about Lucas, do you think?" I said.

"What do you mean?"

"What if you found five significant moments with Lucas?"

Jonathan's face suddenly relaxed. He seemed about to cry.

Jonathan easily recalled five important moments in his relationship with Lucas — and they were poignant, important and full of possibility.

For at least three weeks straight, Jonathan wrote about the friend he had lost. He wrote freely, with no anxiety, and it seemed to relieve him. He wrote about their friendship, Lucas's decline, the day he heard the news of his passing. He wrote from his heart — and it was beautiful.

At least once a session, what he wrote or what he described to me, moved us both to tears.

As of this moment, the essay is not 100% complete, but here is what he has to date. I include Jonathan's free writes after his essay, some with questions I asked along the way to encourage him to expand and flesh out his ideas. This may help you get a window into Jonathan's process.

"Can I doodle on the back of your paper?" I asked Lucas. He said sure, and let me draw trees and mountains over it while he doodled on another one of his sheets. It was one of those small events where despite the fact that memories fade, I will always remember that moment. I took the drawing home with me to color in. I have been coloring in the details of his life, and of his death, ever since.

It was hard to imagine someone I loved attempting suicide, which is why I mocked the idea at first, assuming it was just a sick joke. The moment I learned it was no joke, I sent Lucas a text, hoping that while lying in the hospital, he would read it. I wrote "I love you, bro" and "please get better" in succession. I didn't realize it at the time, but even though his vitals had stabilized, the electricity in his brain had stopped flowing. He wasn't just in a coma, he was gone.

The days following Lucas's death, I desperately wanted to talk to him. I wanted to speak with him out in the air, somewhere private, because I was worried about how my parents would react if I spoke to someone who is dead.

We had felt that death wasn't something we would face for many years, and had treated it as such. I didn't notice him quitting crew, or his grades slipping, or that he was always quick to make a joke about suicide. I always thought he just thought that the concept was so abstract he thought it was funny, though in reality, it was his go-to joke because he thought about it so often.

I had missed his death because I was on spring break in the Caribbean. In the morning, I went out to the beach and rented a paddleboard. The wind was still and the waves light, and I paddled out a few hundred feet. It was just me floating on the most massive body of water on the planet. At this point I decided to lie down on the board, and in a period of near absolute silence said, "Hi Lucas." I talked about my day, and I let him know that I hoped he was doing all right, and that I loved and missed him. I had no idea whether he was there listening to me, but I wanted to say it, because if there was any chance that he could, I would want him to know he was still loved and missed. I lay there for half an hour, and when I finally stood up, I was a half mile away from shore. My paddleboard was at most 50 feet from coral breakers with high waves and a dangerous seabed, and I was continuously drifting towards it. With only one paddle, I tried to turn the board around and paddle towards shore, and for a little while, I was making strides and got around 300 feet closer to shore. I was still very far away, but it was progress. Then, as my arms gave way, I gave up. My paddleboard realigned facing away from shore, and I started to drift back. My first idea was that I had to keep paddling through the pain, but it was too much and the most I could do was to stay in place. My next plan was to dig the paddle into the rocks until my strength recovered. The clear water showed that the rocks were about five feet deep, more than the paddle could reach. However, the waters refraction damaged my perception of depth, and in actuality it was deeper than 15 feet. I was out of plans to save myself, and the closest boat was at least a quarter mile away. So I did the only thing I could do, I stood up on the board and yelled as if my life depended on it, because it did.

For 20 minutes, I floated with my arms waving as only a few boats had passed, and none close enough to hear or take notice of me.

60 feet from the breakers, a motorboat riding along the edge of the breakers saw my hands in the air. He attempted to pull up next to me, but even with the adrenaline, I was too close to the breakers. At this point I couldn't even turn the board around, and was now paddling directly towards them. He maneuvered the boat between me and the breakers, leaving about 20 feet between me and a rocky death.

If I had died that day, our deaths would be closer related than it appears. Lucas's suicide was due in part to his overload of work combined with the stress of the world around him. He drowned in the problems that surrounded him, and so would have I. The only difference was my call for help. Had I not called, I literally would have drowned, and because he didn't, he did. Life is a lot like floating in the middle of the ocean If you don't call for help, the tide will get you, because one man can't fight against the endless tide.

Although Jonathan successfully navigated the waters of his free write to put together this draft, I'm not sure the ending is quite right. He might want to bring in another piece from his free write, possibly his experience creating the paper chain, as a way to speak about the importance of connecting with those you love, even after their death. This draft is a work-in-progress.

Here are a few outtakes from which he may draw sentences or ideas that he wants to add into the draft.

Lucas's mom was the first speaker. I have never been to a wake before, and never seen how the mom of a deceased child usually holds their composure. However, I felt that Lucas's mom's speech was not genuine. The speech was very broad, and the closest emotional attachment I felt in the speech was when she said

"Lucas made me laugh everyday". Besides that, she mentioned that he was loving and caring, but didn't give any details nor go into any personal stories. The speech felt so canned that it could have been pulled off the internet, or transfer from person to person with just the name replaced. Her physical appearance reflected that, as she didn't cry or tear up, and the only hint of genuine emotion was her sniffling, which could have been allergy or sickness related. In contrast, Lucas's uncle stood up, and almost immediately started crying. He reminisced about hikes they took, and how Lucas would constantly keep him entertained with talks about all sorts of politics and science, even on a lengthy 18 mile hike up a mountain. He said that "Lucas would hop up on my back, even though he was 16 and had 20 pounds on me, sending us to the ground laughing hysterically." The love his uncle had for him was clearly genuine, and was much more of a father figure than anyone in Lucas's direct family. It was surprising because out of all the speakers, Lucas's mom seemed the least distraught, as if she felt a burden was off her back. I often wonder if Lucas's mom had been a better mother, and been there for him, if he would still be here today.

It was hard to imagine someone I loved attempting suicide, which is why I mocked the idea at first, assuming it was just a sick joke. The moment I learned it was no joke, I sent Lucas a text, hoping that while lying in the hospital, he would read it. I wrote "I love you bro" and "please get better" in succession. I didn't realize it at the time, but even though his vitals had stabilized, the electricity in his brain had stopped flowing. He wasn't just in a coma, he was gone. The emotions that flooded me preventing my from writing a coherent message, but the message I sent him was from the heart. "I really hope that somewhere in this huge ass universe or another, you can see this. Because I fuckinfnmiss you man and I really want you to know that." I know that it is unlikely he ever saw the text or the countless others sent, but if there is even a sliver of a chance he can see them, I want him to know I haven't forgotten him, even if some months without him have passed. I can still picture his laugh and his smile, as vivid as if he were here right now.

In writing this essay, I was reminded of my paper chain.

Each year of elementary school, I always pushed for a big project during after school care, which I could convince lots of people to help me on. First grade, me and my friends worked on a bus made out of Kinect toys, second grade, a replica of the Golden Gate Bridge, and third grade, attempting to break the world record for longest paper chain. After weeks of work, we achieved a length of over 600 feet on the paper chain, larger than two football fields. The chain was a combination of the efforts of dozens of third graders, and quite the accomplishment, albeit slightly shorter than the world record length of over 54 miles. Despite the fact that the chain was nowhere near any record, it symbolized the great things I could achieve, even at my age, and pushed me to continue on creating large projects and influencing my friends and family to contribute. In the next two years, I would constantly travel down to the basement where the chain was held to give me inspiration to continue working hard. In the last few days of fifth grade, I went down to view the chain, and it was gone. To my surprise, my mom has given it to the school for our promotion ceremony, and the chain traveled all the way from our school to a nearby swim club. The chain created a makeshift path that was vibrant with the colors of the paper and the hard work of the many of the kids who were about to walk it.

CHAPTER 16

Winning the Game

In this time of scandal, people in my profession have had to distinguish themselves from those who have lied, cheated, stolen and scammed to get their students into top-choice schools.

What the scammers have done is demonstrate a decided lack of trust in the student him or herself. In effect, they are saying: You can't do this yourself — the honest way. You have to fool the colleges into accepting you.

This does a great disservice to the mind, heart and spirit of the student.

As Bara Sapir, SAT guru, expresses in her article in the *Wall Street Journal*:

Honor and celebrate your child's success on his or her own terms. Instead of being caught up in a societal tornado that turns children into trophies, ask yourself: What are your child's talents, skills and passions? To be seen and celebrated by you will create lifelong feelings of security and self-worth for your child. Teaching integrity is a better life lesson for children than taking illegal shortcuts.

The journey on which I have taken you is largely an internal one. This journey requires courage to dig deep and stay with it even in the face of fear. It requires self-reflection and honesty, and a big dose of let-go.

Inevitably, a moment will come when you will look at what you've written and have to cut the cord. Because there's a deadline, at some point you have to accept the essay for what it is, even if it has imperfections — and press "send." It will always have imperfections. Even the greatest works of literature have imperfections. That's part of their charm.

The entire process of writing is one of letting go, from the moment you leap (like Thing Two and Thing One) out of the box of your preconceptions and nerves, to the moment you accept yourself exactly as you are — "perfectly human" — about to embark on one of the biggest journeys of your life.

Will the essay get you into the college your dreams?

You can never know that for sure.

You cannot control the outcome. You can only put your all into the journey and hope for the best. Whatever then happens, you have to believe it's the right one. You have to trust that. If you don't get into your top-choice school, there must be a reason. Your first business partner, your husband or wife, your future best friend awaits you at another place. And remember, you can always transfer. I did. It was the best decision of my life.

My experience has shown me that a compelling, authentic, beautifully written essay that the Ad Com reads from first word to last usually does the trick.

In this case, too, you have to let go to forces beyond your control — demographics, competition, the whim of whoever reads your essay, maybe even karma or fate.

But you'll have a whole lot better chance if you free yourself to write from your heart.

At the end of *The Inner Game of Tennis*, Gallwey speaks about what it means to truly win the game:

> *Victories in the inner game… may bring valuable rewards which are more permanent and which can contribute significantly to one's success, off the court as well as on. . .*

I hope that when you are "stuck," in writing or in life, you will trust your associations and intuitions, allow them to flow, and thereby slip through "the low door in the wall that leads to the enchanted garden."

May having read this book help you, off the court as well as on.

I leave you with a beautiful little essay by Miranda Dickerman. You can feel the freedom in her writing; it's almost palpable. At the end of this essay, she lands on perhaps the most important prize of all — self-discovery. *That* you take with you wherever you go.

"Why do kids come here? There's nothing to do," was what a representative from an organization of Jewish camps said visiting Camp Tawonga, where I feel strong and beautiful and whole. It's in the advertisements, on the website, on my counselors' lips — kids come to Camp Tawonga because there you are your best self. Although I am always missing the breeze in the redwoods and the traditions that I love, I don't feel the hole in my heart that I used to when I was away from camp.

It's sunny June in San Francisco and I'm gardening with seven-year-olds in a vibrant, organic oasis amongst industrial warehouses. I'm at the Southwest Community Center chasing three-year old Bismarck who is running and dancing to pop music and yanking me across the cement, eyes fixed on the Caltrain tracks, unwaveringly hopeful for a "choo-choo" to pass by. Behind the glass doors, his mother hugs Judge Kelly because she helped her regain custody now that she is sober and ready to give Bismarck the love he deserves. I see the hope in their eyes and my chest warms.

I'm holding my brother's hand on the bus, I'm composing a song for my violin. I'm running in the forest, I'm prepping for a debate, I'm laughing with my best friend, puzzled over setting up our tent.

I have learned that being my best self is not dependent on location. I don't need to be at camp to be my best self because I am my best self when I am open, learning, and I can see the love within other people and feel it in myself. I'm my best self when I feel helpful, grateful, and in the present. I find joy and love in places I never knew I would ever find myself. My best self is ready to fight against the incomprehensible injustices that I see in the world and stand up for what I believe in.

"Oh my gosh!" my dear friend Frances says, her red nails picking away at the netting covering the bush. "There's blueberries," her eyes shining. We pull the light and chalky berries off the bush. I have never seen something so perfect. I'm taken aback that nature has created this. I think of the canyons and forests I have explored and of those that I still haven't. The sun is shining onto the bricks of the garden and we talk about "how lucky we are" to have each other and to be girls who are as thrilled as anything to eat one delicious blueberry on a glorious June day.

I close my eyes and envision myself and my friends. We're living out our childhood fantasy of owning a farm and raising families together. We run a library. A pre-school. A home for refugees. But maybe we're cities or worlds apart and only talk over Skype. I'm doing research on genetic diseases or studying upside down catfish and saving habitats. I'm a social worker. A senator.

An entrepreneur. There's an unfathomable number of paths that I may follow, and I am excited rather than scared. I am learning to be a woman who follows her heart and seeks help when she needs it. No matter what path I take, I will find joy in helping others, and I will remember how to find happiness and pride. I will surround myself with people who make me feel lucky.

I can think of at least one moment from any given day that I wish I could fit into this essay. There's a baby on the corner, and the bus driver smiled today, and we are alive. It is always worth the extra moment it takes to remember that you're surrounded by beauty. I am infinitely lucky to have a life that has given me the time and space to embark on this journey of self-discovery.

BREAKTHROUGH ESSAYS

Read a thousand books, and your words will flow like a river.
— Lisa See

Through others we become ourselves. — Lev S. Vigotsky

Before I ever picked up a racket, I secluded myself in our den, turned on the tube, and watched Guillermo Villas, Bjorn Borg and the great tennis stars of my time running from side to side across the screen whacking that tiny green ball.

I actually ran back and forth myself, between the bookshelf and the sofa, imitating their strokes.

By the time I stepped on the court for the first time, I already had tennis in my body.

Gallwey explains this phenomenon in his book: "The benefits to your game come not from analyzing the strokes of top players, but from concentrating without thinking and simply letting yourself absorb the images before you. Then, the next time you play, you may find the certain important intangibles such as timing, anticipation and a sense of confidence are greatly improved, all without conscious effort."

So, too, with writing. For me the turning point was reading the poetry of the Romantics. I also had a breakthrough in high school when we were asked to imitate the style of Holden Caulfield in *Catcher in the Rye.*

Reading model essays is a great way to get into your body ways of thinking and articulating, cadences, registers of language, uses of imagery, metaphor and voice without having to analyze them with your conscious mind.

One doesn't learn to speak in a vacuum. In fact, one needs to imitate in order to learn.

Imitation is not only the highest form of praise — it's also one of the greatest and most under-utilized tools for learning.

Great painters often imitate the work of great masters. It is the same with writers.

As a young New York City Poet-in-the Schools, I remember being taught by the poet Kenneth Koch how to teach students who had never written poetry to write poems.

One method he shared was using the beginning of famous poems as starting points. He would read a poem aloud, say, "The Red Wheelbarrow" by William Carlos Williams:

so much depends
upon
a red wheel
barrow
glazed with rain
water
beside the white
chickens

Then he'd direct an entire class to start the poem with the words "so much depends upon."

Though everyone's poem began with the same phrase, they were all completely unique.

(What Koch also taught, using "The Red Wheelbarrow" specifically, is that in writing, as in life, really so much *does* depend on so little.)

The words we use every day (mostly) were already there when we got here. No one has cornered the market on language.

Most students have never even seen a narrative personal statement, let alone been taught how to write one. So it's good to read some.

I am always amazed by my students' responses to the model essays I share with them.

"Wow," they often say. "I didn't know you could write about that!"

Or, "That's pretty wild! Did so-and-so get in?"

I like to show them that the field is not only large but infinite, so they can play in it and find a path that is truly their own.

College essays can be about almost anything, as you will see from the array of essays following.

In previous chapters, I've annotated the essays I provided. The following essays I will let speak for themselves. I chose these from hundreds of excellent essays written by students with whom I've worked over the years. If there is no prompt preceding the essay, assume it is a response to one of the Common App prompts or "Topic of your choice."

These essays are the artifacts of a journey much like yours. I am honored and moved to be able to share them here.

When Mother forgets an important date, such as her own anniversary, I gently remind her with fresh flowers in the kitchen. Over the last several years, she has lost a significant portion of her muscle control and short-term memory. I do what I can to help her, and though I may not understand why she never told me about her illness, I respect her decision.

For nearly half a decade, I've been a silent observer.

I trace my decision to keep silent to a moment in which I was looking through our refrigerator when a tinted bottle reflected the pale, fluorescent light in a manner that whispered emptiness. Though I certainly didn't claim to be a culinary expert, I understood that Worcestershire sauce had no place in Persian cuisine. Curiously, I opened the bottle and revealed a supply of pills and needles inside — that's when everything clicked.

I was never given "the talk" when Mother became ill. I assume that she made a decision not to tell me about her fight against multiple sclerosis. But what frightens me most is that I cannot discern whether Father and Brother know, or whether they, too, are conspiring in not telling me. I wonder if I am truly the only person in my family who has discovered Mother's secret.

The most difficult moments of my day are those when I hear her collapse on our hardwood floor. Isolated behind my poker face, I pretend not to notice because I understand that the most painful part for her is not the fall itself, but rather witnessing a son watch his Mother struggle. Every day, I suspect that we are colluding together in this game of hide-and-seek — except that we're both hiding.

Mother raised me to be an inveterate optimist; my name, Omeed, translates as "in hope of a better future." But there is no known cure for multiple sclerosis, and I know that as her condition worsens, she will eventually call the bluff that I've been sustaining for so many years. My family has always prided itself on honesty and transparency, but much like that opaque bottle of Worcestershire sauce — in stark contrast to the spice bottles of Persia —my Mother's secret seems to conflict with the moral foundations upon which I've been raised.

Often I wonder if there are more secrets that Mother has been concealing, and whether they are as momentous as her illness. More importantly, I wonder whether she is aware of my hiding act and is reciprocating with her own masked oblivion. Perhaps in the midst of this dance, what we are not saying to each other, rather than causing us to float apart, brings us together as nothing else could.

Omeed Ziari, *Yale University*

The University of California: *Describe your favorite academic subject and explain how it has influenced you.*

A mountainous landscape at sunset. One snow-covered vertex emerges above all else, and several lesser peaks slice through the cloud layer below. The lazy evening sun beats down, a dark orange ball in descent. This scene was created in my final project for Descriptive Geometry, my favorite high school class. I drew out the intersections of three cones to represent mountains, warped planes to represent clouds, and a sphere to represent the sun. This combination of geometric forms came together to represent the Sierra Nevadas, a place I've always been fond of.

Descriptive Geometry involved studying the three-dimensional intersections between solids, and then representing them on paper. The class stretched my mind with complicated concepts, but also gave me the freedom to design my own projects and use my artistic skills. I now see shapes in the world around me with a kind of vectored, X-Ray vision. The palm frond on my walk home from school is broken up into numbered elements. I see pieces in a board game as simple intersections of a cone and a sphere.

Despite being harder than most Honors and AP classes I've taken, Descriptive Geometry isn't counted as an Honors class. But never before have I been so happily stumped. I asked my brain to comprehend things I thought were impossible, and to find a solution I had to think outside the box (or rectangular prism).

Descriptive Geometry recalibrated the way I think; I learned that there is more than one way to view my surroundings. Looking at the world through my new geometric lens, I discovered patterns, which I realized I could unearth in every other subject if only I delved deep enough. I had a breakthrough in my perception of the physical world, so why not in the world of language, or the world of music? Within my personal spheres of understanding exist infinite refractions, alternate versions of my preexisting notions. They hide beneath the surface, just waiting to be uncovered.

Niko, *UCLA*

The University of California: *Describe an example of your leadership experience in which you have positively influenced another, helped resolve disputes, or contributed to group efforts over time.*

In his book *A Passage to India,* E.M. Forster writes, "The world [...] is a globe of men who are trying to reach one another and can best do so by the help of good will plus culture and intelligence." Though Forster doesn't specifically mention leadership, he describes the human drive to connect, and the mechanism for doing so. Understanding how to connect in a productive way is the key to becoming an effective leader.

Like *Looney Tunes'* Tasmanian Devil, the song shaking my friend's basement is fuzzy, fast, and energetic. I'm hitting a G power chord, channeling punk rocker Tom Morello. Suddenly we drop into a bass groove, and I'm John Scofield, my fingers sliding over the frets in a jazz swing. Playing with *Thrice Rice* is visceral, and beautiful; though we're performing in front of a crowd, it's like we're the only three people on Earth.

Along with these raw moments comes logistics. I coordinate our gigs, make decisions for the band, calculate our budget, and cooperate on rehearsal schedules. Having spent several years running many of the band's functions, I've learned a lot about leadership. I've led our three-person community as well as the community of a whole crowd. From my experience I've formed a set of core principles: In any situation, I believe it's most important for a person to be authentic, passionate, and organized.

Being a leader means using these qualities to unite a community towards a common goal. Real, authentic, good will is imperative. The crowd feels it when my whole self is in the room with them. It creates a positive feedback loop; as much as I show love to the crowd, they show it back, and we create a better result for everyone. A leader with good intentions inspires their community to participate with good intentions. But this good will alone isn't enough. In order to work in harmony with a community, a leader must understand its cultural roots. To most people, their culture is everything they're passionate about: their morals, their traditions, and even their food. Finally, a leader must use their intelligence and organization skills to solve problems in the community and innovate towards successful solutions.

Moving forward, I'll remember the days troubleshooting in the basement with the band, as well as the nights working with the unique dynamic of the crowd. I enjoy being the leader, and I'll continue to take on more leadership roles as my life goes on, keeping the wise words of E.M. Forster tucked in my back pocket. Wherever I end up, I'll maintain these principles I've come to trust, connecting with more and more communities towards achieving my goals.

Niko, *UCLA*

Tulane University: *Please describe why you are interested in attending Tulane University.*

Their trumpets are in the air. A grinning swarm of people floods the street, dancing to the melody of *Second Line*. One man in a white suit jacket conducts this mass of musicians who have walked out their front doors to join the parade. They march through the streets of New Orleans, the crowd expanding with every passing block. The parade culminates in a huge park, where the partygoers all stop and cheer as the trumpets belt out a grand finale to the song. Within seconds, they've started up with *Caledonia*, and they're on the move again. I'm watching this from the back of the jazz band room on the TV. I've never seen anything like it before. I picture myself on a float, making my guitar wail as I feel the sheer weight of the music consume me.

I'm drawn to Tulane by the excitement of the city and the versatility of the university. My interests are represented: I can see myself becoming a jazz guitarist, an architect, and a food connoisseur all at once. My experience at Tulane will be a launching point for me as I become someone who can change the world, and enjoy myself while doing it. I love that Tulane emphasizes hands-on learning, working with the local community, and undergraduate research. As a musician, I also love the idea of performing right out on the street with my band. Tulane is a colorful place, unapologetically loud and incredibly fun—spicy. I want to jump in with the raucous crowd and become a part of the living, breathing, singing, community that is Tulane and New Orleans.

Niko, *UCLA*

Barnard College: *Pick one woman in history or fiction to converse with for an hour and explain your choice. What would you talk about?*

As any photographer knows, behind every image is a story: Driving home after a month in the California fields, Dorothea Lange felt compelled to stop at a pea pickers' camp in Nipomo, California — "following instinct, not reason." There, she recounts, "I saw and approached the hungry and desperate mother as if drawn by a magnet. I do not remember how I explained my presence or my camera to her, but I do remember she asked me no questions."

Like Lange, I am magnetically drawn to the photograph for which she is most well-known. And this attraction raises questions I wish I could ask the photographer herself: You note that the woman asked you no questions. Ironically, you did not ask her anything in return. Did you take the picture because you, a mother and a migrant, had questions for this migrant mother? Perhaps the photograph itself is the question?

Capturing images relies on instinct. After all, you only have a moment. Viewing photography is also instinctual — why, out of all images, is this the one that drew me?

Then one day, half in sleep, I realize that that woman in the photograph is *my* mother — high cheekbones, dark hair, and deep eyes. When I first locked eyes with her, I was overcome with a sense of familiarity.

As three layers of the story are intricately wrapped into that one photograph — the subject's, the photographer's and the viewer's — my question for Lange would be: Who is the mother?

Mira Kittner, *Barnard College*

Barnard women seek to make a difference in their community, whether through the residence hall, classes, clubs, volunteer work or a part-time job they hold. Describe how you make a difference in your community and what you have learned from that experience. In what ways do you see yourself contributing to the community at Barnard, inside or outside of the classroom?

In a world that is constantly begging us to turn outward, I discovered from a young age that there is also great wisdom in going inward. I often find myself at depths that others aren't familiar or comfortable with. "To walk inside yourself and meet no one for hours," as the poet Rilke describes.

In a strange and surprising way, this turning inward motivated me to turn outward. Once I was at peace with my own ability to question and change, I found a profound interest in holding space for others to do the same.

My leadership and engagement with community reflect a desire to go with other people on a journey. This has taken the form of three weeks at Seeds of Peace in dialogue with teens from the Middle East, and last summer on the Bronfman Fellowship, reflecting on and questioning my Jewish identity. In the past year, I organized an Interfaith dialogue for local teens, attended the Student Diversity Leadership Conference with high schoolers nationwide, and joined the Student Advisory Board, implementing anti-bias and diversity education in our school.

The thread that weaves the mosaic of these experiences together is what I believe to be the foundation of leadership and community: the ability to get quiet, go deep, and speak out. Leadership starts on the inside — it is a state of being, a way to carry oneself in the world — within the walls of the classroom, rippling through the community, in ever-widening circles, at Barnard, and beyond.

Mira Kittner, *Barnard College*

"I can't find *anything* to wear!" I complained, staring straight into the abyss that is my closet.

"The clothes spilling out of the drawers seem to tell me otherwise," my dad chuckled.

I needed a dress for a night at the San Francisco Ballet. Here was a moment for me to step into the most elegant version of myself I could imagine.

My dad piped up. "Did you think to ask Grandma?"

My grandmother was quite a mover and shaker in the 60s. She ran for Congress on an anti-Vietnam platform, was on the Board of Education in the state of Michigan, raised three boys, and did her fair share of world-traveling. Her experiences (and clothes) were the perfect recipe for just the type of dress I needed.

Although ninety-six — my grandmother now has dementia — she remembers her gowns as if she wore them yesterday.

"Yes!" I cried excitedly. "Perfect!"

The gown was stunning: gold and white, floor length, with a square neckline and gold detailing along the bust.

"This is a very special gown. This is the dress I wore when I met Madame Mao."

Pretty soon, my grandmother drifted off. Perhaps she was remembering herself on her grand tour of China, dignified and socializing with political royalty.

Three months later, I stepped out of the car at the San Francisco Ballet, biting wind striking my face with certainty, the shimmering gold circles of the gown billowing in the breeze. I felt like a whole new person. That was the magic of the gown.

Who do I want to be? I thought. I decided that Secretary of State was a good choice for tonight. I took off my gloves to taste the finger food and talked to a ballerina. I waved to my newfound security guards (although they were only men in suits) and cackled with my parents about how absolutely divine it was to be alive. I walked up the aisle to my seat carrying myself like a dignitary.

It was not until after the ballet that I realized it is not the ball gown that allows me to enter a higher realm. It is me. I am the only one who can do that, though the gown may give me extra courage to pursue my wildest dreams.

After the extravagant gala, I challenged myself to take this feeling of invincibility elsewhere, to places where I could make tangible change, where I could freely give my passion and devotion to a project, where I could create beauty. When I was afraid to speak to my peers about a club I was starting, I put on my ball gown (albeit in my head). Likewise, as I was sitting in the waiting room, preparing to talk to a potential big-money donor for the California High School Democrats, I donned my spectacular gown. Sometimes in order to make the biggest change we only need the smallest detail.

When I met Bill Clinton (in real life) at a campaign event for Hillary, I was wearing a red satin dress with cap sleeves that matched Bill's tie.

"We look like dance partners!" he said, shaking my hand.

That night, I was the next female president, meeting my predecessors — Hillary, Barack, and Bill.

The question *what do you want to wear* translates to *who do you want to be.* The gold and white gown is only a metaphor for imagining myself where I want to be, manifesting my dreams.

My grandmother gave me more than just the gown; she paved the way for a career in politics and showed me that the fabric of my dreams is one that I can weave myself.

Rose Miller, *Wellesley College*

Harvard: *Topic of Your Choice*

Let the beauty of what you love be what you do. Rumi

Sitting with my circle of friends at the Farmer's Market, sweet sunshine cascading down my face, surrounded by love and laughter and friends, is beautiful. It is important. Who would I be without discussions about the Trans-Pacific Partnership, Vedic astrology, the best way to study for a test? Without the Zumba teacher showing us the moves, my joy at returning the favor with impromptu West Coast Swing? What is more beautiful than humans being raw and vulnerable and joyful together?

I have beautiful moments every time I am in City Hall.

Looking at the city council members I think, *What if this were me?* The passion and the reverence I feel for our process of governing is beautiful. I introduce Voteat16 to our local legislature, knowing that this is the right thing to do. Lobbying for this measure at our state legislature, testifying at a committee hearing, educating myself, staying up hours to read about the minute differences in the prefrontal cortex at sixteen versus eighteen, ensuring I can justify lowering the voting age. What is more beautiful than self-governance?

Beauty is when I ask my grandmother, ninety-six, with dementia, "Tell me about your life." And man, what a life! Sitting on her couch, my arm around her as she looks through photo albums, she recounts her time as a nurse in World War Two: "I remember meeting your grandfather. He was the handsomest doctor of all, and he was single!" They got married after dating for two weeks.

I sit and soak up her words as if my life depended on it. My life *does* depend on sitting in her living room on a cold winter's day listening to her talk for hours about how to run for Congress (she did) and why bipartisanship is best (she knows). Looking in her eyes, the ones we without question share, I see myself reflected in them. We smile, hug, and laugh.

Beauty is in the students I tutor during lunch. They are always afraid and embarrassed that they need help. It breaks my heart to watch them come in, see their friends in the library goofing off, and then shuffle to the peer tutoring room. But this isn't what is beautiful. Their passion, creativity, determination and vulnerability are what is beautiful. They come in every day to share with me their struggles, and I love to listen. We commiserate about how frustrating trigonometry can be, but by the end of our five-week session, they walk out with smiles on their faces. They take initiative and stand up for themselves. All I have to do is explain a few details to them. This is beautiful.

Beauty is marrying my two best friends, looking out on the crowd and seeing tears. It is a little blurry because, wait, I must be crying, too. I bind their hands and ask:

"Do you promise to love each other for all eternity?" They both nod, unable to speak.

Beautiful moments bloom as I celebrate my birthday on the California coast near Point Reyes, soaking up the sun despite the chilly wind. My parents and my aunt belt out a rendition of *Happy Birthday* that only my family can sing, sand blown into the cake. In between discussing nuclear non-proliferation and laughing over the grit in our mouths, a deep sense of satisfaction resonates in me. This is what life is all about. Being with loved ones and helping others.

My life's work is to create as much beauty as possible, for as many people as possible. My life's work is to spread beauty and spread love, through legislation and social change. For a political junkie, classical guitarist, ocean-loving girl from rural California, I want the chance to make the world, in ever-widening circles, more and more beautiful. What is more beautiful than that?

Rose Miller, *Wellesley*

Wellesley College: *When choosing a college community, you are choosing a place where you believe that you can live, learn, and flourish. Generations of inspiring women have thrived in the Wellesley community, and we want to know what aspects of this community inspire you to consider Wellesley. We know that there are more than 100 reasons to choose Wellesley, but the "Wellesley 100" is a good place to start. Visit The Wellesley 100 and let us know, in two well-developed paragraphs, which two items most attract, inspire, or energize you and why. (Not-so-secret tip: The "why" matters to us.)*

Surrounding me was a wall of solemn and powerful, larger-than-life portraits of the former presidents of Wellesley. I immediately realized they were *all women!* The enthralling tour ended in the majestic Lulu. Looking up at her jagged corners, the many shades of layered brown, I noticed another oddity: there were no right angles in the building. *This is female power*, I thought, *this is female ingenuity.* Women think outside the box, or in this case, outside the lines. What I saw was the true nature of women: we are strong, creative, and fearless.

And they were fearless, my group of political neophytes. The journey started with a plea for funds to take students to the state capitol. Although I got a lot of no's, I got just enough yes's to make bus reservations. As Chair of the California High School Democrats, it was my responsibility to make sure students had the opportunity to be civically engaged and make a tangible impact. Finally, there they were, these aspiring young politicians gazing over the whole expanse of the Capitol building. I saw a bit of trepidation in their eyes. I gave them a look of reassurance, one that said *I'm here to support you. This is going to be great!* It was on these very steps I met one of the most famous Wellesley alumnae, Hillary Clinton. The lodestar of my political aspirations, she showed me how to be a resilient and intelligent leader. During that life-changing meeting I looked over her shoulder, just a momentary glance, at Wellesley in my future. And now, with stoic determination, my posse walked in. Calm and assured, I gave them a thumbs up: *You can do this, too.* And they did. Their courage was beautiful. I watched as they went up and spoke about their personal experiences. *"We deserve to afford every woman the right to choose her own destiny,"* they argued. My group of California High School Democrats walked out of the Capitol building, grinning from ear to ear. A few months later, we heard that the resolution passed. I hope someday to be looking the other way: from Wellesley to the steps of the United States Capitol. Though there may not be a right angle in Lulu, there is an intersection, like that between my love of politics and my desire to help fellow women succeed. This intersection, like going to Wellesley, is the structure of my dreams.

Rose Miller, *Wellesley College*

The University of California: *Think about an academic subject that inspires you. Describe how you have furthered this interest inside and/or outside of the classroom.*

I could spend days at the aquarium. I am awed by the upside-down catfish, which look like catfish but are smaller with a cheetah print. They swim belly up to catch prey near the surface of African waters. I'm eager to use two fingers to gently rub the legs of a starfish and even more excited to hear about the oldest ocean life forms discovered.

I have been inspired by AP Biology from the pages of my textbook to the dark walls of the aquarium to the valleys of Northern California to the yellow flowers in the sidewalk cracks that survive against all odds. I've come to understand the vastness of nature's provisions and I cannot find the intricacies of life to be anything but miraculous.

I want to share my amazement and help others find it. Hearing girls at the local elementary school say that they thought the reason there are fewer famous women scientists than their male counterparts is that women aren't as smart as men, and hearing a mom say she didn't know there was a gender disparity in STEM fields, showed me that my presentation about gender inequality and female empowerment in science was worthwhile. I am in my element as a camp counselor outside of Yosemite and the outreach chair for a nonprofit that brings girls on wilderness adventures. Knowing that each insect plays a vital role in the ecosystem, that the design of these leaves and these wings are intentional, and that the three billion base pairs of my DNA allow me to walk this trail — this is what motivates me to appreciate, learn more about, and share my passion for this natural world.

In the face of a changing climate, I see scientific learning and care for nature as more important than ever. I've spent dozens of wonderful hours studying the complexities of cells and genetics, but the most important lesson I have learned in Biology is that I will forever live my life as a lover of and voice for this enigmatically extraordinary planet.

Miranda Dickerman, *Colorado College*

The University of California: *What would you say is your greatest talent or skill? How have you developed and demonstrated that talent over time?*

From a quick nod to a hand squeeze to unbridled laughter, we are always communicating something. As I have gotten older and gained confidence and self-awareness, I've grown into a thoughtful and compassionate communicator. I am not afraid to speak my truth because I know I have the power to do so with grace and eloquence.

I enjoy taking the time to mindfully plan out a response or share my opinion or vision. I'm forever an optimist and using considered and intentional language to communicate allows me to spread positive spirit without being condescending or irksome. I have learned that it can take so little to spread a feeling — a smile, a remark, a look, a hug — the duration of a mere second can change someone else's whole day.

A good email is underrated. Sometimes it's a few adjectives, a warm greeting, or subtle commentary that changes the entire nature of a message. I'm happy to edit an email for my mom, or a text to my friend's ex-boyfriend, or a friend's email to a teacher. I have learned to communicate my determination and effort to teachers, and when I am struggling, I am not afraid to explain why I think this may be, and ask for help.

Good communication is the foundation not only of companionship, but of good politics and diplomacy. An idea is worthless if you can't communicate its virtues. Bills are passed and people are lost and hearts are broken as a result of poor communication. Parliamentary debate and Model United Nations have been amazing places for me to practice communication and learn from others. I've learned to consider each word I say and the impact it may have, and I am rewarded for my communication skills by deep, lasting friendships, quick connections with strangers, and the seemingly tangible diffusion of joy.

Miranda Dickerman, *Colorado College*

University of California: *Beyond what has already been shared in your application, what do you believe makes you stand out as a strong candidate for admissions to the University of California?*

I'm in the garden and six-year old Johanna pushes a strawberry that had just been in her mouth into mine before I have time to react. The damage was done, so I smiled and said, "Delicious." We are sucked into the magical world inside of the worm bin. I am the happiest, freest and most fulfilled when I positively connect with and help people. I am passionate to go after change that I care about and fight against injustice.

My hunger for learning could never be satisfied. I am fascinated by the red anemones in the garden, moved to care about the natural planet, and enthralled by the relationship between species. I am equally stirred by my class discussions about *Invisible Man* and *One Flew Over the Cuckoo's Nest*. I am just as engrossed in our US History debate about whether Andrew Jackson is a hero or not. I am a driven intellectual thrill seeker and I will bring my hardworking spirit into the classroom and contribute my insights, curiosities and passion.

I close my eyes and envision myself and my friends. We're living out our childhood fantasy of owning a farm and raising families together. We run a library. A pre-school. A home for refugees. But maybe we're cities or worlds apart and only talk over Skype. I'm doing research on genetic diseases or studying upside down catfish and saving habitats. I'm a social worker. A senator. An entrepreneur. There's an unfathomable number of paths that I may follow; I am excited rather than scared. I am learning to be a woman who follows her heart and seeks help when she needs it. No matter what path I take, I will find joy in helping others, and

I will remember how to find happiness and pride. I will surround myself with people who make me feel lucky.

Miranda Dickerman, *Colorado College*

University of California: *What have you done to make your school or your community a better place?*

I have found immeasurable joy engaging in the communities that I love. I grew up in The Mission of San Francisco, a vibrantly diverse cultural neighborhood. As I came to understand the complexities of this place that I love, I began to want to contribute.

At the Homeless Prenatal Program (HPP), women give and receive support to our neighbors via case management, parenting classes, knitting workshops and more. Most employees were previously clients and as a volunteer I've discovered how special it is to work amongst people that I admire. I've never been more inspired than by the brilliant, open-hearted women at HPP. It is they who move me to go after what I want, fight against injustices, and be an active member of our neighborhood.

Learning from the unafraid women in my life and seeing congressional committees and board rooms full of men inspired me and a friend to give back to the community of women that we are so proud to belong to. I love leading Girl Up, a club that works to empower girls locally and internationally. I've learned that I thrive as a leader and I've found fulfillment and pride heading letter writing campaigns, presentations, movie nights and bake sales.

I've made dear friends in the kids I've tutored at the elementary school blocks from my house. Seeing students in my classes at school struggle because English is their second language and knowing the magic of reading moved me to be a literacy tutor. I'm so lucky to see students flourish as they get through *Cat on a Mat* and reach for *Charlotte's Web,* and I want to continue to help children follow their dreams and be comfortable in their skin.

I've learned that we have something to learn from everyone regardless of who they are. Although I don't know what the details of my future career will be, I do know that I want to spread love and compassion wherever I go.

Miranda Dickerman, *Colorado College*

The University of California: *Describe how you have taken advantage of a significant educational opportunity or worked to overcome an educational barrier you have faced.*

Once I took a concentration test on the Internet. The test consisted of images of a city scene or a mountain scene that changed quickly. I took the test multiple times, and each time I scored in the 0th percentile. I had extreme difficulty not clicking when I saw a mountain: I couldn't notice fast enough what I was looking at and couldn't hone my attention in on the image. I took the test on different days, and I saw how my mind was in a million places that weren't where it was supposed to be. I was trying so hard that it hurt, but nothing changed. This experience is a perfect description of the way I feel about my work ethic and focusing skills sometimes.

For a long time, I didn't think much of my difficulty starting assignments and paying attention because I was a very successful student. I thought it must be like this for everyone. It wasn't until my courses got much harder, a few years into high school, and when I learned about how people with learning disabilities can still be good students, that I started to wonder if it was a little harder for me to do certain things than for others. Since that time, I got diagnosed with ADHD and have received different kinds of support because I advocated for myself and was able to reflect on my experience and tendencies.

I work on overcoming lack of focus every day. Doing so is satisfying and beneficial, and with time, it has gotten easier. Lifestyle changes, a support system, and daily medication have immeasurably improved my ability to manage my time, prioritize my passions, and focus on my work. I've become increasingly confident in my abilities and motivation and I love to learn. I have so many ideas and passions! I love writing songs to play on my violin and organizing activities for my club makes me want to and feel like I can do anything. I thrive when I'm learning and questioning and loving and sharing. ADHD will always be a part of me. I'm learning to embrace it — and instead of restricting me I will continue to have it propel me forward as an enthusiastic, curious and driven learner and leader.

In school, extracurriculars, and at work at my congregation, I have grown as a leader, collaborator and listener who has seen how special it is to work as an integral team member with people that you admire. As a lover of deep connections, I will venture to be an open, compassionate, and active member of the campus community. As a learner and leader who is curious, driven and passionate, I thrive in a space that provides me the freedom to explore, connect ideas, and grow intellectually and personally.

Miranda Dickerman, *Colorado College*

"Sohan, if I throw a rock in the air, physics can tell me where it'll land five seconds in the future, right?"

"Sure, I guess."

"Doesn't that mean science can be used to predict the future in general?"

"Could that apply to thoughts too?" I cut in.

Shankara stopped in the middle of the street.

"Thoughts are just electrical signals bouncing off neurons. I don't see why not."

I paused. "Wouldn't that make every thought you had predetermined?"

I felt slightly nauseous. Turning away from Shankara, I took in a breath of the balmy night air — rare for this time of year.

If physics can predict my actions, do I have a self? What makes me more than just a purposeless chain of firing neurons? So, I'm an automaton, going through the motions with no authentic reason why? I started to feel trapped by this worldview, almost paralyzed. Because I didn't know what else to do, I kept doing what I was doing, but my life during this time felt like a blur.

One day — it happened to be Black Friday — as I was mindlessly browsing the Internet, still caught in a kind of philosophical funk, something caught my eye: an ad for a drone, with a camera. Only $60.

Could I code it myself?

I felt an unexpected jolt of excitement.

A series of cold calls later, my friend Adiyan and I secured parts for a discontinued model of an industrial drone, the 3DR Y6. Two months of scouring cryptic wiring diagrams, developing person detection code, and battling with an annoyingly spotty wireless connection went into hacking together a drone that would supposedly fly.

It was time to run a test flight.

"Is the camera on?" I asked Adiyan. He nodded.

I hit "enter" as I bit my lip, running the code on my computer that, theoretically, would tell the drone to take off, rotate to search for a human being, and land in front of them.

A still minute of silence.

I approached the drone. Two and a half feet square, heavy, it could move at a max of 65 miles per hour. It felt like I was approaching a wild animal. My hands tentative, I disconnected the battery and exhaled a breath I didn't know I was holding. Time to try again. And again.

It seemed like it would never get off the ground.

Around this time, I was working on a scene from Arthur Miller's *After the Fall* at the Lenaea Theater Festival, with my partner, Didem. Shivering in the dark, we sat facing each other, repeating our lines outside a hotel.

"Look me in the eyes. You have to let me in, Sohan. The only way we win is if this scene is real!"

She was right, but that night I couldn't take the risk. At 4 in the morning we called it a day, more frustrated than before.

Maybe it was the previous night's repetition, or the pressure of performing the scene in front of judges, but the next day, as I looked into Didem's eyes and acted as if I loved her, I felt the currents of true emotion. As my character walked away from hers, leaving her screaming on the floor, I felt wrenching guilt. I felt *alive*.

The words I said were scripted. Rehearsed. But unbelievably, in that moment, I felt genuine love.

The next weekend, Adiyan and I went back to the field, determined to give the drone one last shot at flight. We restarted with a fresh battery.

The unnaturally loud buzzing of the propellers scared me, but my heart flew up with the drone as it finally rose off the ground. The drone felt like its own being. *It* felt *alive*.

As for our drone, he also got off the ground, and here he is, filled with authentic purpose, curiosity, and love, writing to you.

Sohan Vichare

For months, the same dream: A man follows me down the street. He walks faster. I throw my bag at him and miss. He pins me down; I know he is going to rape me. Then I wake up.

In December of 2016, my friend Charlotte showed me screenshots of a group chat, "Let's rape a girl this weekend...in the back of a pickup truck. Let's rape Dani." All of the texts were from boys I had known for years.

"What should we do?" I asked.

"I don't know," Charlotte muttered.

I felt nauseous. The bell rang. I ran to class. Directly in front of me sat one of the boys in the text thread. I could smell his cheap cologne: sickeningly sweet, like mint, cinnamon, and sweat mixed together. My mind was racing. Maybe I had misread something. Was it a joke? Would it be better or worse if it were a joke? I sat there, barely listening.

Later that day, my friends and I discussed what happened, and it became clear that everyone had been harassed by the boys.

"He pressured me to have sex."

"In class he whispered that he wanted to fuck me while I was sleeping."

"He faked orgasms in my ear during biology."

"He hit me when he was drunk."

This brought into focus a pattern of abuse and misogyny that had been going on for years. We decided to go to the principal.

"I am taking this very seriously," the principal said. "We have mishandled similar cases. I don't want to do that again." I left her office feeling worse. As we walked across the courtyard, the bitter winter air whipped around us. The last bell rang, and students flooded out of the buildings. One of the boys waved at me, and I quickly looked down. What would happen when they found out?

Soon after, two of the fourteen boys were suspended. They received their suspension three days before winter break, essentially an early vacation. The others retaliated with verbal and physical threats. I began to fall behind with my classwork. On top of that, one rainy morning, I slipped running to the bus and got a concussion. When I returned to school, I decided to transfer into the Independent Studies Program. I needed a fresh start.

After a month of hounding the Berkeley High administration, we finally began Restorative Justice. Working with the Restorative Justice facilitator for two months prepared us to meet face to face with the boys. In the culminating circle, the boys were apologetic. We said our piece. I was relieved, but I knew there was more work to be done.

Dani and I decided to make a documentary about sexual harm at Berkeley High School. The first girl we interviewed passionately explained how media perpetuates rape culture and how Berkeley High should invest more in sex education. But when we asked if she had experienced assault, she was quiet. "I was raped." As she spoke it became clear that she blamed herself. Almost every girl we interviewed said similar things. Dani and I left every interview completely sobered. The sad part was, as one girl described, "the aftermath of rape is just as traumatizing as the actual event." The school and justice systems systematically disenfranchise victims. This disparity grows for women of color, queer, and transgender women. I have been catcalled, groped, harassed, and threatened by men, but I have never felt as powerless as these women.

I now have a new dream, one to replace the nightmare. I never thought my interests and possible career paths would lie in Restorative Justice and Gender Studies, but last year's events gave me the courage and ambition to stand in my own power and help others do the same.

Tara Blossom, *Sarah Lawrence College*

Six-hundred and fifty words represent only a minute of what my life was like for five months. A million vivid snapshots of the pain I woke up to everyday.

"We just want to make sure we're getting rid of ALL of it," my oncologist said. I soon figured out that this was code for "We're about to give you the strongest, most toxic thing you will ever put in your body."

I told everyone that it felt like my stomach was a pretzel twisting tighter and tighter. As the pretzel became more intertwined, the grains of salt would grind against each other causing pain to ripple through my body, but no one listened. "Don't eat dairy!" they said. "Avoid gluten." "Anxiety," they concluded. But I knew it was something else.

With each new round of chemo injected into my body I got a little more pale, lost more weight and more hair, and felt a little more life being sucked out of me. It seemed like I was a sand castle, grain by grain, slowly being blown away by the wind. Finally, I looked my dad in the eyes and said: "I want someone to shave my head right now."

I used to wake up every morning to a wave of pain. It was like my brain turned on right before my eyes opened and that wave of pain came at me from all angles. My throat felt like nettles were stuck inside of it. I could feel each organ in my body pushing itself to function, overexerting with each breath, as I desperately clung to consciousness. I could see myself slowly deteriorating when I needed to be strong for my family.

Shaved, my head felt so light and clean. No more thin strands falling whenever I turned my head. I was liberated, and I took back control of my body. In that moment I realized I looked just like the girl I had seen by the elevator months before: pale, bald, gaunt, and frail. I had become that girl.

I saw white fluid slowly making its way through the tubing that lead to my heart. I felt a chill ripple through me as the liquid began to spread through my veins. Soon my eyes got droopy. Then, completely black and fuzzy. After a few seconds, the voices began to sound like echoes as they were engulfed by the black fuzz. I could still hear the beeping of the machines as everything else faded into silence.

"Honey, I don't know how you've been handling this so well. You're being strong for us all; you're my hero." I could see the tears forming in my dad's eyes, which made me cry also. That was when I knew I had to pull it together. I could do it. I just needed to take it one day at a time.

It took five months for me to physically recover from Stage 3 Burkitt's Lymphoma. I went through the most strenuous time of my life physically and mentally on my journey to recovery. At moments I felt like everything around me was crumbling and I had to be the one to hold it all together even though I could barely hold myself up. I would wonder a lot, why me? What could I have possibly done to deserve this? What I came to believe, however, was that everything happens for a reason, and getting cancer happened to me for a reason. Surprisingly, at moments during this period, I was the happiest I had ever been. Almost losing my life caused me to discover what is truly important — positive human relationships — and what I want to do with my life, as a nurse, is support people the way I was supported. I see now that the moments I've shared with you add up to what was my life, and what is now me.

Gianna Gunier, *UCLA*

There's no feeling like dancing perfectly in time with the many rhythms of the loud, powerful *djembes and dunduns*. You can't think about it, you have to *feel* it. The drums tell you what to do — how to move, when to switch movements, where to go, when to stop. It is essential that you hear them within your whole body in order to do West African dance. This type of dance is more than just an art form, it is a way to communicate and connect with other people, a celebration of life, and a way to preserve African culture. When practicing West African dance, dancers don't only learn the moves, but also their meaning and the cultural context behind them. I have done many dance forms in my life and only in my African dance classes do I feel like I am becoming one with the music and truly letting go. It is my ultimate form of release and self-expression.

Often being one of very few white people in my African dance classes puts me in an unusual position. I could feel like an outsider, but because I am deeply committed to this dance form and to celebrating the culture from which it comes, I have been embraced by the Bay Area African Dance community, in and outside of Berkeley High.

I make an effort to immerse myself in this community every opportunity I get. In addition to my class every day at school, over the past two months I have danced at an outdoor festival in Oakland, attended a West African Dance conference, taken adult-level classes every weekend, become a certified drum circle facilitator, attended two African dance performances, and performed at a celebration of the 50th year anniversary of the African American Studies Department at Berkeley High.

Recently, I have had the honor of being asked to dance with my teacher's elite adult company. When it came time for our final dance, the members of the company bowed their heads to me; I could see excitement and approval in their faces. My heart ignited in my chest. We took off and blazed a trail across the dance floor. We weren't just dancers, we were light, we were a fire burning at full intensity, we were life.

I feel the drums everywhere. When I'm not in class dancing, I'm playing rhythms with my pencil on the table while doing homework. Or I'm sitting by the window in an English class hearing the beats from the dance room carried across the courtyard by the breeze. No one else in the class hears them. They aren't as acutely attuned to that sound as I am. The drums are my pulse, coursing through me all the time. The drums are within me.

Nicole Bordeaux, *UCLA*

Brooke became the sister I never had before I knew I had one that I lost.

Every night, we set the clocks one and a half hours ahead to 8:00 PM, exactly my twin brothers' bedtime. "Chase and Christian! Bedtime!" hollered Brooke, our *au pair* from New Zealand. Once the twins were in bed, Brooke and I settled down in front of the TV to watch *Fringe*.

Despite having their own rooms, I still find my twelve-year-old twin brothers, Chase and Christian, together in the same bed every morning when they wake up. They have the same friends, play the same video games, and both love reading. Their only difference is one looks three years older than the other. I sometimes wish they actually were three years apart. Their unique bond as twins leaves no room for me.

At moments, I imagine them floating together inside my mom, underwater, with me standing outside on the shore.

Hidden from me was that I did have a sister, but she died of a heart defect shortly after birth when I was three. Her name was Kate. It slipped out of my mom's mouth in front of my friend one day when I was fourteen. This made me angry: How had I never heard of her before? Why would my mom let me know in such a casual way? Hours later, the shock stabbed me. I imagined a different life, a life in which I had my sister standing next to me on the shore.

A few years later, at the Southwest Regional Rowing Championships, I dragged my arms in the water as my boat crossed the finish line seven seconds ahead of our rival, Newport, soaking everyone in front of me. Jack Woll, a few seats ahead of me, threw up his arms in celebration. Minutes later, we approached the beach. Then, out of the blue, our coach dove head first into the water with all of his clothes on to congratulate us. All eight of us followed suit and jumped out of the boat and into the water, together. There we were, almost as if being baptized together, the crew, my crew, my adopted brothers.

Even though I will never be able to get my sister back or squeeze between Chase and Christian who live their lives in sync, I have found others to sync up with. Every afternoon I go to the boathouse and practice with seven other teammates. We row in unison: our hands flow as one, our legs thrust as one, and we share the passion to win as one. We trust each other more than anyone else in the world. Just as Chase and Christian formed their bond underwater inside my mom, I form my bond on the water with my crew. This challenge has made me stronger, giving me the faith and courage to know I can find and create a family wherever I go.

Andrew Stoddard, *MIT*

I had known my phobia was unusual when even the esteemed "Index of Phobias" could not identify it. Was it rooted in my unusually high sensitivity to citrus? Or did it bring back a painful memory from my childhood? In fact, I had never even tried an orange. However, after losing a high stake bet with the president of the Public Speaking team, I was forced to choose between jumping into (the shallow end of) a freezing cold hotel pool at 3 am or taking a bite. Drenched and trudging through the hotel lobby, I couldn't help but feel as if I had made the wrong choice.

Whatever it is within me that keeps me from eating oranges (a stubborn but illusory aversion) has also prevented me from exploring an important aspect of my identity.

"Actually, Steinberg is a German name, not a Jewish one," I have often heard myself saying.

"Stein and Berg are like the two most Jewish names I've ever heard," is a common reply.

"My grandfather lived in Germany and when he emigrated he had to change his na... You know what?" I said, interrupting my own defense. "I don't need to prove to you that I'm not Jewish— I know who I am." But the truth is, my own sense of my identity is complicated.

You're only Jewish if your mother is Jewish by Orthodox law. Or am I Jewish purely based on the complex methodology of "Steinberg sounds pretty Jewish to me, bro." Each metric yields a different result. Yet, even without a definite answer, I still feel a sense of guilt when I reject my Jewish identity.

One day, my debate partner Zac said, "You should come to temple with me." But before I could reject his suggestion, the sincerity in his eyes stopped me.

So there I was at Temple Isaiah for the first night of Hanukkah. The potato latkes were crispy, flaky and comforting. The conversations were engaging, the choir was beautiful, the *derasha* was inspiring, but this isn't the place for me, I thought. Although I had believed my own argument against organized religion, in the absence of direct opposition, I lit a candle, ate a latke and my chest lightened.

I wish I could say my Hanukkah adventure broke through the shell of my defenses. Not so. I was once again forced to face a mighty opponent in 10th grade PE. There I stood, a nearly six-foot-tall high school student splashing around in the shallow end with a collection of pool toys. Upon my arrival to PE the following day, I was launched into the deep end by my classmates. The water consumed me, the world went black, and at that moment I was convinced it was all over. But as I thrashed from side to side, the water gave me a warm and forgiving hug, as if to say that it was all right that it took me seventeen years to learn how to swim. After that day, would I consider myself a proficient swimmer? Not even close. An average swimmer? No, not really. But what I did learn is that there is a certain amount of comfort that comes with being out of control, and once I embraced that, I allowed myself to go with the flow.

I saved the toughest opponent for last. The spherical monstrosity whose name strikes fear into all that hear it... the orange. My hands were shaking, I was sweating bullets, but this time it was different. I stared squarely at my opponent and I actually said aloud to the orange: "Your reign is over!" I peeled open that bad boy and took one juicy bite. With my enemy vanquished, and conquest concluded, I can officially say that I do not like Oranges, but at least I can say I gave it a shot.

Evan Steinberg, *The University of California, Santa Barbara*

"To be a pole vaulter you have to have three very important qualities. Got that?"

"Yes"

"You have to be smart; I know from your mom that you are. You have to be handsome; you're fine there. And you have to be fast; we'll see about the fast part, won't we?" I started practice a month later.

"Remy, look how skinny you are. What do you weigh? Eighty pounds! You need to put some meat on those bones!"

"I know what you need — you need gym and protein."

"What about friends?"

"You have to make friends with the pole!"

And so I began my career in pole vaulting.

"Remy, I've told you this for three years straight, and every time you make the same mistake," my coach Roger admonished. "I just want you to get upside down!"

My life had already been turned upside down just a few years earlier.

I was visiting my grandmother, tie-dying shirts in the garage with friends, when Jeremy's girlfriends says, "It's OK. You can pet him; he doesn't bite."

Taking her encouragement, I reached out to pet Face, a cute pitbull who was sitting on his haunches idly observing me. The next thing I remember is writhing on the ground, his maw clamped around my left forearm. From here on I recall the events in a mix of first and third person. After I was in Face's grasp, I recall him dragging me through the side yard and into the garage.

From my grandparents' house I was rushed to the hospital. To put it mildly, the thirty-minute wait was the second most painful experience in my life, the first being when the doctor had to administer a numbing agent into each laceration in my arm via a hypodermic needle. Once the pain medication was administered,

I immediately passed out and woke up in the hospital the following morning.

Directly after the incident, I lost all dexterity and experienced serious nerve damage in my left arm below the elbow. I could barely touch my fingers to my thumb and could not move my wrist at all. A touch to my arm depending on the location would either be completely imperceptible or cause excruciating needles of pain to course through my arm. It took one year before I could fully extend my fingers to high five friends, another before I could make a fist, and another before my strength fully returned.

Once I had the strength to get myself aloft, the thought of letting go of control terrified me.

"I know, I know," I said to Roger. "All I have to do is jump backwards, flip upside down, and try not to fall straight onto my face. . ."

I hear some friends behind me yell out, "Run like the wind!" I laugh in my head and focus. I set my hands onto the pole; I set my feet at the right position; I set my mind to the task."

I blast forward, not counting my steps. I rely on pure muscle memory, trusting my legs, arms, and body to do what they're supposed to do.

"Butt to the sky! Point your butt to the sky!"

And to my surprise I do.

My legs continue to rise over my head, my arms pulling my body vertical alongside my pole like a leaf caught in the warm updraft of a summer breeze, and as I extend, I glide effortlessly over the bar and free fall to the mat.

I set the bar high for myself and have built the strength and tenacity it takes to keep surmounting whatever challenges life throws my way.

Having undergone such physical trauma, I have gained empathy for those experiencing debilitating injuries. While I cannot know the extent of any person's struggles, I can and readily do empathize with their struggle, sharing whatever encouragement I can.

Remy Feru, *The University of Texas, Austin*

"Come on Jamie, let's get on the plane!" My uncle pleaded.
"But I want the one with circle windows."
"That plane isn't going to Oakland."
"I don't want the rectangle windows!" I exploded, just shy of a tantrum.
I was completely inconsolable.

I don't know if it was the windows, or it was my four-year-old mind wrestling with the recent accidental overdose of my mother Shannon, the windows a catalyst for my volatile reaction. One day I was cuddling with my mom, admiring her bright red hair and infectious laugh, watching Popeye. The next day, she was dead.

With just one plane ride, I left behind everything familiar in my life: my half-sister Caitlin and the stories she read to me. I left behind the fields of dry yellow grasses that had an aura of golden light after lunch. I left all of this to go to a place called Oakland, to live with my Uncle, and his boyfriend Fernando, both of whom I had never met. I also left behind a life of hunger, abuse, and uncertainty, for a life full of opportunity, stability and aspirations.

I don't know what my Mom's life would have been like had she lived. I do know she was my only consistency. Unlike my dad, who was seldom around and often in jail. One day we would play hide and seek, the next day, I watched through tear-slurred lenses as he hit my mother, leaving me wondering who he really was.

I don't know how the pain of losing someone can be quantified in such a way that two deaths are comparable. There is no set of numbers, no volumetric flask, no Geiger counter that can show the intrinsic value of a death. I do know that I heard my very soul rip in half when I learned that Draven, my friend and choir mate since fifth grade, died in the Ghostship warehouse fire. News of his death sounded like the heavy, dense silence after the last note of Samuel Barber's *Agnus Dei*. Without a doubt, my mother's death created an immense hole in my heart. I lost her, but a whole new world opened up for me. Draven's death created no opportunities for anyone. It was a void that kept sucking, a gaping hole, yawning ever wider with each passing day.

I don't understand how I dealt with life's hardships and challenges when I was four. I do know that singing gives me a sense of place, bringing me hope, solace, and joy. The intense, invigorating piano motif in Schubert's *Die Erlkonig*. The solidarity between the choir and orchestra in Mozart's *Requiem*. The guttural discordance of Britten's *War Requiem*. The beauty of the myriad unknowns that make the human experience unique in Rachmaninoff's *Vespers*, Berlioz's grandiose, omnipotent horn section in *Te Deum*.

Drop the jaw. Engage the breath. Raise the soft palate. I am completely in shock as my body automatically prepares itself to sing *Loch Lomond* at Draven's funeral — the song our choir sings every summer sending off seniors to adventures unknown. Now we are singing to mourn the end of his adventure, to say an irreversible goodbye, to cherish our brief time together.

The somber music picks up a mystical quality, creating worlds with merely a handful of notes. I exhale and more than music comes out — my eyes, envious of the liquid tones of my mouth, send a small river of tears trailing down my face onto the wood floor. Gazing into the puddle of tears, I see the gap between Cameron and Andrew, where Draven should be. We begin the journey of mending our hearts, the only way we know, we sing.

"... By yon bonnie banks and by yon bonnie braes
Where the sun shines bright on Loch Lomond
Where me and me true love were ever wont to gae
On the bonnie, bonnie banks of Loch Lomond..."
James Applegate, *Yale University*

"Shreya, look."

My friend Kashish pointed to the sky. It looked like a painting with streaks of blue, purple, pink, orange, and yellow, hastily smeared across it. The result was a breathtaking image that we stopped in our tracks to admire.

We were breathless, but after one look over the hill, it was all worth it. We could see our entire city from up there: the valley, the clustered houses, and the multicolored sky. There was our school, our park, our grocery store. Everything—my problems, my stresses, my worries—seemed so small and insignificant from up there: It was one of those rare moments where everything felt right. I was in my element.

But I don't always feel this way. Sometimes a restlessness takes over my body. I feel like I just can't settle, like I'm sitting on a tiny sharp rock that bites into the back of my thigh. A hummingbird flutters in my chest wanting to get out.

When I started with dance, I thought, "This is it! I found my calling."

I felt the same way about basketball, soccer, and debate. Then one day, by surprise, while I was helping a terrified new swimmer get into the water for the first time, I felt a sea change happening inside me.

Henry's eyes were red and slightly puffy. The sound of his cries filled the arena. Clinging to his mother, he buried his head in her arms as if trying to block out his worst nightmare. It was clear he wanted nothing more than to leave. Manager after manager tried to comfort the boy, offering him plastic figurines, foam bananas, and silicone rocket ships. But still, he refused to get into the pool. I watched the instructor frantically struggle to bring order to her class. Her brows furrowed and her eyes looked to me as if in a desperate plea: "HELP!"

It was my first day on the job as a teacher's assistant, and no amount of training could have prepared me for the chaos of that moment.

"Hey big guy, is this your first time coming to swimming class?" I asked. "It's my first day too."

Hearing these words, Henry's head turned out of his mother's arms. He looked at me, still scared, but now his eyes perked up, almost incredulous that I was in the same boat as he.

For a few moments, Henry forgot his fear of the water. As if testing to see if anything would jump out and bite him, he finally, hesitantly, poked his toe into the pool of uncertainty.

The chaos of my first day that initially frightened me turned out to be just the type of chaos I needed. Every thirty minutes for four hours, I would be responsible for teaching a new group of four students, each with their own unique set of skills and levels of comfort. Every thirty minutes was a new challenge: one time it was helping the kids learn to breathe, the next time, it was teaching them to stay afloat. These challenges inspired me to think on the spot and multitask. In this job, I didn't need to seek out variety, complexity, and challenge—it came to me instead. Those four hours were completely and utterly chaotic, but I loved it. As soon as I stepped out of the pool after each shift, a wave of calm washed over me.

For me to be happy, I'm going to need fast-paced, ever-changing challenges that morph in front of my eyes. I don't mind chaos. In fact, I thrive and feel most in my element, in the uncertainty of unknown waters.

I know I can trust myself and the decisions I need to make by what I feel inside. If I feel like I'm on top of that hill watching the sunset, happy and free, I know that's the right path to follow.

Shreya Puli, *The University of California, Berkeley*

Bard College: *In 250 words or less, how do you imagine yourself living and learning at Bard?*

Ever since I was little, I've done school differently. I went to Waldorf kindergarten, I was homeschooled for 1st and 2nd grade, I went to a Montessori school for 3rd and 4th grade, then I went to public school for 5th grade. For middle school, I attended a local public school in Berkeley, and then I traveled around the world with my mom in 7th grade, studying online from Nepal, India, Thailand, Italy. I went back to public school in 8th grade, and since then, I've been in Berkeley public schools. In my junior year, I went into Independent Studies, and now I'm on track to graduate early.

I have always designed my own curriculum and I have experience in different learning environments using various modes of learning. Because of this, I am seeking a multidisciplinary education where I can combine my interests in Anthropology, Gender Studies, Psychology, and Sociology. Also, concentrations such as *Science, Technology, and Society,* or *The Mind, Brain, and Behavior* are fascinating to me because they are in-depth studies in subjects I want to further explore. I hope to pursue a career as a psychologist or sociologist, continue to make films, and perhaps one day work with battered women using Restorative Justice and therapy as a way to move past trauma.

Why Bard? I can't think of a better place to walk my own path in an environment where individuality, collaboration and innovation are not only supported, but encouraged.

Tara Blossom, *Sarah Lawrence College*

"94% / A Stay after class! In bold red letters, this was written at the top of my test. I rifled through my chemistry exam. My definition for the law of conservation of energy read: *"Rien ne se perd, rien ne se crée, tout se transforme."*

Half a page in my test was written in French.

Speaking four languages does have its drawbacks — I sometimes find myself thinking in the wrong one. I tend to replace Spanish words with French and Chinese with Spanish.

Why do I know more than my fair share of languages?

Because I am a mutt. My great-grandparents were a Spanish-speaking saddle-maker in a Saharan oasis, a Prussian draft dodger, a Hispanic trader in the Cape Verde Islands, and an Irish farmer. I come from Catholic, Jewish, Protestant, and animist stock.

My blood is not the only puzzle in me. I was raised in a diverse community in Berkeley, California (I left when I was eight). I lived in Italy, and studied in conservative Catalonia (Spain) and liberal France before moving to the Midwest, where I now live in a homogeneous and conservative culture, often as the only child of non-Anglo-Saxon descent in my classes. I speak three languages at home (Spanish, English and French) and one more on occasion (Mandarin, which I learned in daycare and have studied since).

I have been a part of so many cultures that I don't fit any mold. I am not a jock — but I study in a sports-oriented high school, where I was player of the year for my soccer team. I am not a geek — but I am the webmaster for my school parents' organization. I am an ardent environmentalist with liberal ideals — but I am part of the national gold medal team in scholastic pistol shooting. I want to be an engineer — but I love to write creatively. I spent most of my life in cities, but I live in farm country, in the middle of a forest, and I work as an equipment mechanic at the farm next door. I write poetry in French. I publish a website about energy storage because I am passionate about fixing climate change. I star in a YouTube video, eating tripe to win a bet with my uncle. I love chemistry, but astrophysics fascinates me, and psychology is engrossing, while anthropology amazes me.

My nomadic roots could be to blame for my wide range of interests. Yet they are my greatest strength. I have befriended people who speak many languages, come from various cultures, and have diverse social upbringings: I can relate to everyone and get along with anyone.

Without ever pushing myself forward, I can make a group get along and function well together, socially, for work, or as a team. This ability is my most valuable skill. I draw compromises and make all feel valued. I repair what links break down across the group; I bring humor when anger starts. I use words, silence, gestures, atmosphere, jokes. I encourage the one, cajole the other, push for a better understanding. I make sure we cross the T's and dot the I's, and I pick up any task that falls through the cracks. By connecting with everyone, I connect them with each other.

I am a good scientist — yet there are many better. I am a good writer — yet many have more talent. I am a good athlete — although I will probably never be a world champion. But the mix of cultures, languages and people that make me who am I have forged into me a unique skill: I help whatever group I belong to work in concert, and efficiently. How strange it is — what should have fractured me into so many pieces has made me whole.

Cameron Thouati, *Stanford University*

Stanford University: *Stanford students possess an intellectual vitality. Reflect on an idea or experience that has been important to your intellectual development.*

It was hard for my parents to convince my brother and me to move to the Wisconsin countryside from sunny California. We became enthusiastic only when we realized that we could ski to school over the thick layer of snow typical of the prairie winters my mother saw growing up.

But we never saw a stable snow cover that year, or in the six years since. On the path to school, across the fields, I look down over my boots, into the mud. I hate mud. Not because of its color, or its texture, but because it shouldn't be there. In its place should be crisp, clean snow under my soles and on either side of me, piled up on the standing corn straw. Instead, the dead stalks look like dirty, pockmarked chopsticks drowning in a sea of brown.

Since our move to the muddy winters of snowless Wisconsin, fighting climate change has become my favorite daydream, almost an obsession.

Every day, sun, mud or snow, I think as I walk: CO_2 scrubbing? Solar power? Nuclear fusion? What will reduce climate change? What is the future of energy? Do we need to mine asteroids? Build colony ships to escape a dying Earth? Why is progress so slow?

Climate change has driven more than my walks. It has inspired my readings, interests, college plans. My direction. I must help create the future. Maybe I'm naïve to think I can, but that accursed mud drives me to try. It is a challenge I can't ignore.

Cameron Thouati, *Stanford University*

Step by step, origamists like myself layer onto an ever-changing square of paper new features, shapes and creases! A plane will soon become a jumping frog, a deconstruction of biological life and wonder, a simple cluster of cells waiting to be molded. The first few folds are the most primal cellular layers: the endoderm, the mesoderm, and the ectoderm. As the beast grows, it becomes lifelike and magical. I'll deconstruct the world, rebuild it again, and call it Life/Art.

One piece of paper can be a crane, a tractor, a dragon.

Driving down the bumpy Ring Road in a tricked out Icelandic camper-van, my brother and I enact strategic chess wars. We fight to control the most important turf (the center), sweat to parry off constant checks, and relish in the despair of hanging pieces. Then we harken back to last Christmas, which we spent in an English Pub across the Thames, inspiriting the wooden pieces, watching the bartender prepare to lock up. Every chess game is distinctly *alive* and unique and enhanced by the atmosphere in which it occurs. The relationship between chess and origami? Blank slate becomes turf war. Sometimes it is best to have a knight and a bishop, or bishop and a rook, or simply a lowly pawn creeping up his queening square.

As part of the community that is Instructables, we all embrace a give and take relationship, exchanging bits of knowledge, techniques, and projects. I post tutorials on location tracking Weasley Clocks, photogrammetry, IOT devices, and casting molds. I enter contests; and then I judge them. Instructables' radically diverse community has even compelled me to submit tutorials on lucid dreaming and coconut butter popcorn — topics far from my usual electronic interests.

I'm a creative chess player, origamist, *maker.* My mode of creativity? Seeing the life in the inanimate. I revel in inspiriting wooden chess pieces, paper sheets, and electronic components.

There is no secret guide to comprehending, exposing the ebb and flow of life. One can only try to recreate it, let it run wild, and then sit back gazing upon it.

William DeGroot, *Amherst College*

The University of California: *Think about an academic subject that inspires you. Describe how you have furthered this interest inside and/or outside of the classroom.*

I found myself in a private lecture, face to face with: " $a^2 + b^2 = c^2$."

"Know this one?" my professor asked.

Of course I did, but what I found mind boggling was the assumption that a theorem like the Pythagorean can be true in every case, let alone entirely provable.

In that moment, I was confronted with something sublime and exciting: Mathematics. Everything physical, and magical, and even electronic, seems to have origins in this discipline.

So much was I taken with this passion that I immediately made arrangements to take Pre-Calculus online during the summer of 10th grade — a fast track which eventually allowed me to finish AP Calculus BC (the most advanced of my school's math courses) as a junior. I was then free to take on even bigger challenges in math. Alongside an AP Statistics course, I am enrolled in Discrete Math this year, in which I study a thrilling collection of introductory proof techniques. These courses have taught me about the ways that propositional logic and p-values are being utilized in the cyber realm. This schedule also allows me to tutor senior students currently enrolled in AP Calculus BC. The 48-inch whiteboards in my living room are now littered with partial proofs and enchanting graphs!

This past summer, I did statistical research at Sonoma State University alongside Assistant Professor of Computer Science Mark Gondree. As part of our research into statistical randomness testing, I used Python scripting to analyze the efficiency of pseudo-random number generator (PRNG) tests. Dr. Gondree was mainly interested in the outputs of the PRNG tests when they were fed with biased (non-random) data. I learned about biasing datasets, developing comparable graphs and tables, and proving the optimality of biasing algorithms. In other words, I wholly embraced my fervor for mathematical exploration.

The letters and symbols which live on my whiteboards and in my mind inspirit me always. The opportunities I've had, the research I've conducted, the epiphanies I've experienced, have cultivated my numerical aspirations. A future of endless, playful experimentation simmers.

William DeGroot, *Amherst College*

The University of California: *What would you say is your greatest talent or skill? How have you developed and demonstrated that talent over time?*

There is the face of the bewildered spectator after an unnoticeable undercut; there is the mirrored solemn gaze of the king; and there is the grin of the magician, who just performed his flagship trick. Magic is about finger dexterity, misdirection, engineering and mathematics. More than a specific field, it's a conglomeration of the unexplainable. A skill with uncountably many faces.

In magic, an unassuming object which possesses a secret function is known as a "gimmick." Performing and creating magic allows me to revel in "making", experimenting with the physical and electronic, with Arduinos, lathes, and 3D printers. I love to manufacture my own gimmicks and have been doing so since I received my first magic set at the age of five: gimmicks as simple as a double-sided playing card or as sophisticated as a vibrating pen which communicates to me — in Morse code — recent tweets which tagged my account — the latter an idea I'm currently pursuing in my Project Make class. The ingenuity and technological familiarity I've developed in programming camps and microcontroller contests lend themselves beautifully to the art of magic.

But this is not to discount my infatuation with card magic, a discipline centered around "clean" tricks — non-gimmicked effects. Here, two techniques are in play: fascinating displays of mathematics and strategic sleights of hands. I just can't get enough of the cyclic, mathematical patterns (like *Si Stebbins* orderings) which dominate stacked deck effects. And I adore practicing false cuts, Faro shuffles, and back palms. Stressed out from an impending test or satisfied with the completion of an arduous project, my meditation is fondling a "Bike" (or Bicycle branded deck).

I've always been attached to wonder. It's such a fickle feeling, and it's always been at the helm of my decision making. It's my whole life: inducing, investigating, finding, and creating magic in the world around me.

William De Groot, *Amherst College*

The University of California: *What have you done to make your school or your community a better place?*

As "A," I grip my tattered, cardboard letter and step onto the stage.

I smile at R and T. Together we spell out the name of our beloved town, G-r-a-t-o-n, CA — where community matters.

The other letters and I hold hands, sidestep across the platform, and bop our heads in tune with the eccentric MC's catchy chant. Slip N' Slides glisten; hay bales compose quaint sitting areas; a "Welcome to Graton Day!" banner flies overhead. I treasure my memories of Graton (my hometown): my memories of elementary school field trips to the annual Graton Flower Show and playing kick ball with T and O (and sometimes R) down the street. And every year, I am deeply indebted to Santa Claus, who always finds time to visit the Graton Community Center.

So I preserve and carry forth Graton's beloved traditions. As an elementary and middle schooler, I baked apple and custard pies for the Graton Day dessert contests. I juggled colorful spheres or jammed on my Uke for our talent shows. I read Christmas stories aloud to children waiting to sit on Santa's lap.

Now a more capable, aware, high school student, I *give back* in more novel (and perhaps practical) ways. Drawing in hordes of sugar-crazed kids and often donating my profits, I am a staple cotton-candy vendor at Oak Grove's (my Graton-based Elementary school's) *Día de los Niños* festivities. But I still try not to neglect the tiny details. I still storytell to scared toddlers. I imagine a future of children bike riding down our blackberry paths. And I understand the importance of upholding traditions.

I still remember… holding hands with the consonants next to me. Looking out into the crowd. Being part of a larger town, community, word and world.

William DeGroot, *Amherst College*

Winding down our community trail in dark, shimmering raincoats, rain pouring down, last week of third grade, we catch sight of a delightful group of trees. Risa and I lock eyes. *Treeland* is born.

A lovely patch of shrubbery, Treeland was most loved by us for its plentiful abandoned logs, hardy stumps, and discarded branches/leaves — its construction potential. From these materials, we sculpted teepees, castles, skyscrapers, schoolhouses, dreams.

I don't remember when Treeland slipped soundlessly away. Not sure if it was a certain year or day or moment. Risa and I have grown apart now. The ever-forward flow of life seems to have hidden our tracks.

I *do* remember when I found Treeland again. *Come on Lulu!* I gently tug on her leash and glance upwards. The bushes are overgrown; the trees are frail and dying. The wooden bridge? Rotting. The entire playground of my childhood? Perhaps a tad larger than my 100 sq ft bedroom.

I wonder now: Did Treeland actually change? Or did I?

To me, this ambiguity and subjectivity is what's most important. Whenever I uncover the proof to a theorem or churn out a particularly interesting flourish of words, I can never completely recall the experience. I drift into a trance where memory is banned and ideas are unbridled. I am lost in a moment of imagination and bliss — a unique landscape of the mind that is morphing and changing instantaneously. Neurons fire. Emotions swell. The *real* world fades. Hidden away in Treeland's woods, the make-believe obscures reality and creates *wonder*. I think that's just how creativity works.

And that's how I want to live my life — today, this coming 2019 summer, my time at UChicago, and in whatever comes next

— seeking out this beautiful haze and reveling in its *wonder*ful fruits.

William DeGroot, *Amherst College*

Engineering electronic gadgets (using my mathematical skills) has become an addictive joy in my life, complete with failures and mistakes, until that blissful moment when everything — the idea, the process, the materials — comes together. Finally, I have a 3D-Print of the sound waves created by saying "Happy Birthday, Mom!" (the best birthday present ever!) or a location-tracking Weasley Clock, or even an SMS-messaging doormat.

In the infancy of this obsession, I became entranced with an emerging technology: electroactive polymers (or EAPs for short). Shaped by electricity, EAPs have recently become widely used in industrial robotics — as grippers, fins, and propellants. But, as I would proudly explain to any friend who would listen, EAPs were still largely unavailable for public use! I wanted to bring EAP tech to the "making" market, to Adafruit, to Radioshack. To that end, I emailed a pioneer in EAP technology — Engineering Professor at ETH Zurich Manuel Kretzer — asking for assistance in constructing my first prototype.

Surely, I was thrilled that Manuel ended up providing me with some specific information. But that wasn't the sincere source of my ecstasy. The world, for me, had just deepened. International collaboration!

And yet, somewhere amidst all this electronic excitement, I found myself in a private lecture, face to face with: " $a^2 + b^2 = c^2$." "Know this one?" my professor asked. Of course I did, but what I found mind boggling was the assumption that a theorem like the Pythagorean could be true in every case, let alone entirely provable.

As thrilling as gadget-making can be, in that moment, I was confronted with something even more sublime and exciting: Mathematics. Everything physical, and magical, and even electronic, seemed to have origins in this discipline. The 48-inch whiteboards in my living room are now littered with partial proofs and enchanting graphs! In the midst of an AP Calculus lesson about solid revolutions, I realized that a cone was simply a slanted line rotated around an axis. Then, by calculating the definite integral of a rotated line with variable coefficients it might be possible — I thought to myself — to derive the formula for the volume of a cone: $\frac{1}{3}$ r2.

Interestingly, whether contemplating the calculus of rotated objects or building fantastical electronic gadgets, the place where I can understand most and create best is not my homeland but my *Vietnam reality*. In Vietnam, the land of my stepmother, I tread the liminal boundary between the real and the surreal. Drifting down a river in North Vietnam, I lose myself. Hanging stalactites, moist rocks. The blackness soon ends and our vessel departs the abyss, now edging itself back into blinding light. My pupils dilate and I make sense of my surroundings.

Gazing past the river's coast and into the vast forest I fall into a trance, a murky dream while maintaining an immediate physical connection with my environment. In such a place of magical wonder, appreciating the physical is trivial. While in Vietnam, I keep my kite filled with abstract ideas still fluttering high in the wind but forever tied to the ground below. This is my Vietnam reality.

And it's the place I often find myself: listening to the whir of my 3D printer; twisting some jumper wires in my knuckles; thinking of propositional logic; uncovering the solution to my bonus homework question. Is there a risk of flying the kite too high? Not as long as I don't neglect the pencils I hold nor the fleshy delicate appendage called my hand.

My interests and my future are both concrete and abstract: holographic dreams to be played with by my mind *and* my senses. This lesson is perhaps the most precious gift Asia has ever given me, ranking alongside fried scorpions, spiny (but incredibly tender!) rambutans, and holiday cards from my Vietnamese Nana written in the third-person.

William DeGroot, *Amherst College*

I stroll down dirty streets. I listen to the sweet sound of my grandmother's Puerto Rican accent on the phone. I feel mischievous, so I decide to embarrass my friends. I saunter into a crowded place and beat my chest, pretending to be a gorilla.

When I used to whine about anything as a little girl, my mom would tell me that I could choose to,

"Either turn on the light switch or sit in the dark." It took me a few years to understand that she meant that my experiences are what I make of them.

I climb rocks and gasp at the charm of the Golden Gate Bridge. I sit, nestled in my bed and read my new book about Buddhism. I was not raised religious, but I am fascinated, so I make notes on post-its to stick in its pages.

I watch Gene Kelly dance and pretend that I'm there with him. I get excited when I can book my flights so early that I have to wake up at four in the morning to get to the airport on time.

I challenge myself to find a source of happiness in everything. When I first experienced anxiety as an elementary schooler, I was happy that I developed a unique sense of humor to help me cope with it.

When my dad was jobless for a few months six years ago, I was happy that he was able to spend more time with my family.

I obsessively arrange my food into symmetric designs. I sit in the passenger seat of the car with my dad. We giggle at absolutely nothing and slap each other's arms. I twirl through smoky campfires in the woods with my campers.

The world makes me happy. I make myself happy.

Bianca Rico, *Barnard College*

Within seconds, ash started raining down all around us, in the body of utterly flawless leaves. But that's not what caught my attention. The sun had turned into a fiery red inferno that looked like the menacing eye of a mysterious beast, watching idly as everything around it slowly burned. That eerie sight snapped us back to reality. We ran—the fastest I have ever run—into the main circle, usually the hub of activity, where we saw Lily, a staff member, talking furiously into a walkie-talkie.

"You need to leave. Everyone's already been evacuated. If your parents aren't here, I'll take you myself. Now go get packed. Quickly!"

Moments before, I had taken my eyes off the ground for the first time since the beginning of our hike, expecting to see the familiar outline of trees in the distance framed against a brilliant blue sky.

"Max, do you see what I see?"

I searched for the playful smile that never seemed to leave his lips; the absence of it told me more than words ever could. Time stopped as we stood there looking at each other, frozen in place with the realization that something was very, very wrong. It was 1:00 P.M., the peak of our beautiful, summery Tuolumne day, but the sky was grey. It was a dark, thick and threatening grey that mixed with the reddish hue emanating from all around, a smoky cage that enclosed us. I held out my hand and Max grabbed it and pulled me close, as if we could protect each other from what was to come. Just then, a single leaf fell from the sky, a skeleton, every vein perfectly preserved in the ash of what had once been something vibrant and alive. That was my last year at Tuolumne. The camp burned to the ground hours later.

In all my years there, Tuolumne never lost its magic for me. I never got too old to sprint up the hill in search of my favorite cabin, or shriek and laugh as I jumped off Beaverhead—a rock in the swimming hole aptly named for its distinctive shape. At Tuolumne, I was able to return to the best parts of my kindergarten self. I could make a best friend before the end of the day, be impulsive and carefree. I could wander into the forest and come back hours later without having to worry about work to do or tests to study for. I was someone at peace. As I grew older, this became even more important to me. Tuolumne became my refuge—the place that I would close my eyes and think about when the world at home got too overwhelming.

The sum total of my seventeen years is wrapped up in the essence of Tuolumne—in every makeshift cabin, beaten path, melted ice cream snack. The physical place is no longer standing, but the person it helped me become is still going strong, as are the relationships that I built there. So even though camp is not physically there anymore, its spirit is alive in me and always will be.

But more than that, I have carried on the Tuolumne spirit and translated it into everything I do, and I am proud of how I have let it change me, both in its presence and absence. With the campsite reduced to ashes, I have found more meaning in the community that is still standing. My best friends and I can still go and watch the camp play with the same people we love, even if we are sitting on plastic instead of wood. We still sing the camp songs and go on adventures. We don't need the camp to be best friends. Through all of our late-night conversations, rafting catastrophes, and month-long trips to Europe, I realize that wherever I am, I can be carefree, or whimsical, or adventurous and at peace.

Olivia Sterling-Maisel, *Carelton College*

University of Chicago: *Chicago author Nelson Algren said, "A writer does well if in his whole life he can tell the story of one street." Chicagoans, but not just Chicagoans, have always found something instructive, and pleasing, and profound in the stories of their block, of Main Street, of Highway 61, of a farm lane, of the Celestial Highway. Tell us the story of a street, path, road—real or imagined or metaphorical.*

This is the place I can remember living since birth.

Sometimes I get flashes of a different abode, another time. A white-walled apartment with red oriental wall hangings and white cabinets. Tall chairs, a blue couch with a yellow pattern.

Yet, whatever that place was, it is long gone; here is what I have now. A tan duplex, with a tall lantern in the front yard, petunias, and more petunias.

The road in front of the house was long and winding and cracked and faded to a light blue. As a first grader, the road went on forever and forever, for miles, perhaps even beyond. Who knew where the road ended? Recently, I drove by, and was surprised to see that the road extends for less than a mile. As a child, that same road extended for legions… and in dreams… covered oceans and continents…

In real life, on this road, there were people of all types. My neighbors were Egyptians. Across the street was a builder. Down the road was a boy with "disabilities," just like in my own family. Two houses down was the home of a twenty-something woman who introduced me to movies that she loved. She moved soon after I met her, but I still remember her clear blue eyes. She showed me a small part of the world though her television. A few months afterward, we found ourselves moving to a larger house about three minutes away.

The day of our move, our neighbors waved as we backed out of the driveway. Right, left, a few minutes straight, and we were at our new house. Even though our new house was only three blocks from our old home, it felt like worlds away, quieter and the houses were farther apart, feeling forbidding and aloof. Not long after moving into our new house, we found ourselves on a plane to India, visiting our grandparents. Humid, rainy, hot. India was a familiar place to me. From the moment I got off the airplane and landed in the airport, everything around me had a familiar smell. It reminded me of the smell that came from my father's suitcase after he returned from trips to India, visiting his own parents. Even after I reached the dusty, winding road to my grandfather's house, atop a hilly garden, I could smell spices that were common in my mother's kitchen in Chicago. Paprika, turmeric, chili powder. Smells like home. The dirt road leading to the house was a rusty red, and after a while, morphed into a proper brick road that winded into the open garage. Right next to the open garage was a beautiful garden, full of roses, vines, and old, old trees. There were so many memories surrounding the garden, and the two old mango trees. When I was younger, about eight, there was a flamboyantly blue swing suspended from one of the sturdier branches, and we looked at it with stars in our eyes. There was no better transportation to reach our dreams. Another swing was in the back of the house, but its charm disappeared once we discovered snakes hidden in the bush behind it, ready to strike. The trees were a source of entertainment once the mangoes were ready to gather, and my brother and our younger cousins were permitted to scramble up ladders, grab however many we could fit in a basket, and proudly present them to our mothers. Beyond the small garden and its pristine white wall, there is also a stretch of land that belongs to my grandpa. There are rows of fruit trees and greenery, and you can spy the winding, rusty red road and the gate leading to the outside world of bustling auto rickshaws and street vendors.

It seems like many roads, but it was one road, really, from my first memory, the tan duplex, to this very house from which I write to you now. From a neighborhood of all sorts of people, to plucking mangoes form ladders, every step I took along the way helped give me new perspectives of the world. The road ahead seems unclear from this point forward, however it is mine to walk, and even if it is full of twists and turns, my stepping stones will be the roads my feet have already known.

Surya Nair

One miraculous day, I discovered the paperclip. It was the beginning of a new world order for me. I had begun the summer naively filing my college applications into one single eight-and-a-half-by-eleven manila folder. I thought, "Great. I'll just stuff everything in here." This method worked for about a week. That is, until multiple drafts of essays tangled themselves between pages of applications and the "folder" no longer folded at a single crease. In fact, the folder had become one big crease, losing its rectangular shape completely. It was such mayhem that I would lose items inside the folder for weeks at a time until, as if by some miracle, they would suddenly reappear. Then the day came. I discovered the seemingly simple, twisted world of adult organization. How delicately those metallic tendrils of angel hair clasped to my stacks of papers. My discovery of the paperclip inspired me to invent the "sub-section," where essays could rest within categories in my dilapidated manila folder. That curled strand of genius initiated the beginning of a whole new era in my life—The Era of Organization!"

Cat Hill, *The University of Southern California (USC)*

My gaze was fixed on the trees flying by when I noticed what seemed to be the edge of a frozen lake concealed behind a cluster of bushes.

"Look!" I exclaimed, nudging my teammate, Jessica, in the arm.

A devious gleam crept into her eyes when she noticed the ice, and I knew we had the same idea.

"Let's skate," she said.

One glide forward on a silver blade and I had entered a whole new world. The usual commands "Extend your leg!" and "Tuck your arms!" were left behind as I slipped into this realm of beauty, exhilaration, and flawless simplicity.

Unlike the circular rinks I was accustomed to, the lake seemed to stretch on forever. For the first time while skating, I could hear the chirping of the birds, feel the sun on my skin, taste the biting winter air. Something about the freedom of having no bounds and of being out in nature connected me to forces bigger than myself.

However, as we prepared for the World's Competition the very next day, something was off. I could not keep pace with the music. Instead of the usual ease I experience when skating, I couldn't figure out where to put my feet. Maybe it was the nagging sensation of being trapped indoors after such a liberating experience the day before, or maybe it was the longing to be back at the hidden lake, but before I knew it, I was down. I was rushed to the closest hospital, where the doctor diagnosed the injury as a sprained knee.

As painful as it was not to be able to perform with my team the following day, watching them skate from the sidelines gave me a similar feeling to the one I experienced on the hidden lake. I saw synchronized ice skating in a new light. The arms of twelve girls moved in unison to the beat, every step mirrored to perfection by each skater. They did not seem to skate as individuals, but as one person moving with such serene grace. Watching my team, I imagined myself on the ice as well, our arms intertwined, performing as we had practiced for years. In that moment, I realized synchronized ice skating makes me a part of something bigger than myself and is more than the sum of its parts. When a group skates in unison with the same passion and goals, it becomes somewhat transcendent. Each skater moves not for themselves, but for the team as a whole.

Ever since those couple hours on the hidden lake, skating and even the way I view the world has never been the same. I no longer interpret ice skating as an obligation or even a sport, but as a privilege and a way to be in touch with the natural forces of the universe. The experience also brought me to the realization that there is a hidden lake within me as well, in which I am free and in synch. I love ice skating so much because just stepping onto the surface brings me back to myself and my connection to the world.

Kristy Beiles

"How could you do this to me? You are supposed to be my star!" the little Russian man shrieked, waving my papers frantically in the air. I shrunk further into my chair, fully aware of the stares of twenty pairs of eyes on me. As if I was not already embarrassed enough, Mr. G then proceeded to grab me by the shoulders and drag me to the front of the classroom. I could not believe it. A hot fire boiled up into my cheeks and I fixed my eyes on an invisible piece of dirt in front of me.

"She is my star!" he announced to the class, bouncing up and down so fast on his toes that his cheeks turned as red as the Expo marker in his hand. "She is my star, but she has failed me."

His bushy mustache wiggled around like a worm while he shouted a stream of Russian curse words, and I thought his glasses would fall right off the tip of his nose. However, before I could laugh at this amusing sight, he was calm once again, and returned me to my seat.

"Do better," he whispered, and I could feel the icy sensation of disappointment in my ear.

I was ashamed. Ashamed that I, being Mr. G's star and the best student in the class, had failed him. The itching sensation haunted me for the rest of class, until I vowed to myself that I would rework the set of problems until I had mastered the concepts. I opened the textbook and began reading with a newfound sense of motivation and purpose.

Mr. G had been my teacher since I joined the middle school math club as a fifth grader. I still remember walking into his classroom for the first time.

Immediately upon entering the building, a voice from all the way upstairs could be heard. We climbed the stairs, craning our ears to try to make sense of a loud, heavily accented voice. The sight revealed as we opened the door to the classroom could have been in a movie. A short, comical looking man stood by the whiteboard. He was dressed in high-waisted jeans, a button-down shirt, and a pair of spectacles hanging off his crooked nose. The little hair he had was a mess, and it looked as if he had not slept in days. He flew back and forth across the whiteboard, his pen whirling into a massive blur of letters. Occasionally, he would whip around and jab the pen into the air, his bushy eyebrows furrowing together. My gaze became fixated on a little mole on the side of his mouth that jumped around as he yelled commands at the students. At one point, the buttons on his shirt popped open in the midsection, leaving his plump stomach exposed. To this day, I don't think he ever knew.

Ever since joining the math team at Black Pine Circle in 5th grade, I have been working at an advanced level. When I walked into Mr. G's classroom every day for class, I would automatically go to my private desk in the corner of the classroom and begin working on the math problems that sat in front of me while the rest of the class followed his lessons. Mr. G taught in a way unlike any I had ever experienced. He promoted a creative learning style by using visuals such as geometric models and statistic problems involving M&M's. He had high expectations for his students, and did not accept anything but the best efforts, which is all he got. His methods worked. At lunch, we would laugh at his amusing ways and his funny accent, but when it came time to learn, we all paid strict attention. We were afraid to disappoint him.

From the first week of meeting Mr. G, I knew my whole life was going to change. Math classes became harder and the work began to pile up on my desk, but so did my expectations for myself. Mr. G made me aware of my capabilities in math and also of my capabilities to persevere when faced with challenges. Instead of shying away from difficult problems or unfamiliar concepts like I did in the past, Mr. G made me feel as if they were adventures I had the privilege of pursuing. I began to enjoy the process of solving difficult problems in all of my classes, not only his, even if that meant failing multiple times before I succeeded. Mr. G made me realize that I am capable of more than I give myself credit for.

He is also responsible for my interest in pursuing a career in mathematics. The hands-on learning tasks and interesting set of problems he put together opened my eyes to the exciting and complex world of math. Not only did he open the door to my interest in pursuing a career in mathematics, but gave me the confidence, sometimes the hard way, to believe I could succeed in math and in whatever I attempt to do.

Kristy Beiles

"People are mad," one of my closest friends Lydia said to me, "because you have never been directly affected by gun violence. It doesn't make sense that you get to lead the walkout."

The most common criticism against our gun violence protest was its lack of diversity. Despite weeks focused on outreach, the size and demographics of our group remained the same, mostly white.

"It's not an issue that involves you. It's not your fight," Lydia went on.

"My grandmother died from a bullet wound, remember?"

No sooner were the words out of my mouth than I wanted to take them back. I was filled with guilt for using my grandmother's death to defend myself. All I knew of her death was that she was shot and killed in Michigan by a man who tried to rob her small furniture store. My father was ten; I never even knew her. Though my grandmother is barely ever mentioned in our household, except once a year when we light a Yahrzeit candle in her honor, her lingering memory is plagued by darker connotations of violence and loss. My grandmother's violent death was hard for me to understand and even harder for my father to discuss.

Months after the walkout, I found myself telling a friend how guilty I felt bringing up my grandmother in the context of gun violence. "You have the closest connection to gun violence of anyone I know, and I witnessed a double homicide."

"I never even knew my grandmother. It hurt my dad, but it was too long ago to have any effect on me."

But this wasn't true. From a young age I have desperately tried to understand the loss that my father experienced. I watch his eyes well up with tears while the rest my family gazes at a small flame that burns in his mother's honor. I rarely ask him about her death, because I don't like the way his voice changes when he talks about her; it is softer and full of sadness.

But now, reminded of every feeling that her death has evoked in me, I was forced to admit that, indeed, I have been affected by her murder and that, in turn, I have been directly affected by gun violence.

My time at Oakland Tech has illuminated the blind spots I have regarding issues of race. It has woken me up to and helped me address my "white fragility." And for that I am grateful. But to believe I have not been deeply and personally affected by gun violence is to ignore the death of my grandmother, and the unquestionable impact that that loss has had on my family. It is to believe that my background prevents me from being compassionate, open minded, and a rightful participant in my community. And I refuse to do that.

Lauren Kahn, *The University of California, Berkeley*

University of California: *Describe an example of your leadership experience in which you have positively influenced others, helped resolve disputes, or contributed to group efforts over time.*

Once we sat down to convene the first meeting of Pi Club, the boy handed me a stack of graph paper and a worksheet riddled with diagrams and word problems. Thirty minutes passed as we worked, but not one other person showed up. Still, I returned every Tuesday of my freshman year to a club of two. But the following year, the boy went off to college, which made me the club's lone member and by default the new president of Pi Club. Left with only a club name, I began to spread word of our first meeting by hanging flyers in the hallways and making announcements in every math classroom about the Pi Club's renewal.

On the first official day of my presidency, I bought three "pies," three cans of whipped cream, and printed out a large stack of math problem sheets. After the lunch bell rang and thirty some students settled down, I stood up, introduced myself, and spoke about what our club had to offer. To interested members, I provided a meticulously researched spreadsheet of competitions, offered myself and our teacher advisor as tutors, then began explaining the carefully-developed curriculum that I had prepared weekends before. Of all the visibly excited new club members darting towards the stacks of worksheets before the array of pies, none were more excited by the prospect of a classroom teeming with passion for math than I.

Now president for my third year, I have come to see the true importance behind Pi Club's success. I have created a space that allows students whose interests aren't so mainstream to express their love of math and find others who feel the same. Together they can solve summations, explore conic sections, crack differential equations And now we are a club of forty!

Lauren Kahn, *The University of California, Berkeley*

I walk down one of my city's most populated streets daily. It swarms with people, bustling, as well as crowds of squatting coin gatherers and entertainers. Many of them hold out paper coin cups to passers-by. Every once in awhile somebody pauses to drop small change into the waiting palm, but most walk past in straight, purposeful lines.

If individuals had kindness not only for those they were interested in and cared for, but for others as well, this would be a route toward selflessness. Compassion and empathy are potent forces — how can one possibly move forward and contribute without consideration for others?

I see my vision of the street expanding. Empathy and kindness is not limited to sparing a few dollars to a beggar on the street, to someone, who despite being given the small change, will probably remain at the feet of the passers-by for the rest of their lives. Compassion, in my mind, can become unlimited. The sidewalks will become less populated, not because there's a dissipation of life force, but rather because there's an expansion of minds and, most importantly, of empathy.

I dream that freedom, not perceived as the outcome of carelessness, but rather as the result of boundless kindness, will become the path to worldwide empowerment, equality, and awareness.

Talia Bloom, *The University of California, Santa Cruz*

As a little girl, when I was in nature, nothing was covered with words or explanations, but I still sensed an inexplicable beauty, an indicator of purpose, to everything that I saw. From when I was around five years old, I used to make fairy houses in my backyard. One time a boy in my class told me that the tooth fairy was not real, and I screamed at him that she WAS! The same thing happened with another boy. He laughed at me because I loved fairies and I tried to tell him what I saw in the sky — the little gold sparks so clear against the light blue — and he told me it was just something happening with my eyes. I just could not believe that he needed proof beyond what was so obviously there for me — the absolute certainty that there was magic everywhere and voices speaking all of the time.

I could hear those voices, and they continued to call out to me when I was in nature. I would talk to trees and hug them, feeling the rumbling, rooted and sturdy energy flowing through them. I would listen to the plants speak in their soft, simple voices about invisible creatures and insects and the wind and the almost incomprehensible experience of the plant that I could just *sense*. I listened to the insects and bees, too.

Years ago my family went on a camping trip, and my mom asked me to speak to the swarm of yellow jackets that had been bothering us, and to ask them to leave. "Remember to use love," she said. I walked over to the picnic table and sat down in the midst of the yellow jackets. I knew that they could sting and it would hurt, but I was not afraid. I closed my eyes and listened. I listened to how the yellow jackets only wanted food, and how it drew them to us like some heavenly paradise. I smiled and imagined love forming a cloud around me, spreading outwards to envelop them. I left and ten minutes later when I checked the picnic spot, the immovable yellow jackets had gone.

In these connections with nature, I became aware of spirituality. Although I could not fully articulate it, I knew as a certainty that there was a significance, plan and a reason for everything around me of which I was often unaware. These magical experiences showed me what was unknown, and the knowledge, the sureness, that there was an unknown.

I furthered explored that certainty throughout Jewish day school during prayer time. I learned that when I concentrated hard enough, I could talk to God and feel my emotions vibrating intensely. Later I learned that I could also pray for whatever I felt motivated to bring into my life.

Recently my motivation drove me to practice Judaism in ways that would bring me closer to such a presence, and I decided to explore my religion further though Orthodoxy and deeply intensive practices.

Now my motivation is about the need to be aware of and explore the external world and see how it is reflected in me internally, and how I can mirror the goodness of God's unity with the world's goodness. I still listen to bees and trees, and to whatever magic that goes otherwise unnoticed that is out there. I still speak to nature and am spoken to, and it does not always require a prayer book or a religious ritual. I stare at the leaves on plants and the etchings of the veins on the leaves and I especially stare at the gold sparks in the sky and know that to believe in what is not spoken aloud, all that I have to do is watch and listen.

Talia Bloom, *The University of California, Santa Cruz*

Here is what Talia said about her writing process. It seems fitting to end this book with the words of a student who followed her heart and wrote her way into the college of her dreams.

When I first started writing, I constantly tried to plan out exactly what I wanted the readers to know about myself or the topic. I would guess what their specific judgments would be about my writing, even before I really knew what I was writing about. Once I had an idea that I wanted to portray, I would write my first sentence. Then I would delete my first sentence. Then I would write it again, slightly differently. Then I would delete it. Then I would rewrite the same thing, call it an introduction, and start on my second "paragraph" in frustration. The process was painstakingly long, and while my word choice came across as advanced, my creativity hadn't really had a chance to develop in my writing.

I was trying to write an essay called "How to Think Gratefully." I was intent on making the instructions in my essay clear and succinct, but at the same time descriptive. I got stuck easily with these intentions set, as I was used to explaining concepts such as observation, gratitude, and awe with definitions and examples. It felt nearly impossible to write from the reader's perspective, to write as though I was *describing* someone's *experience* of thinking gratefully.

I had to learn to relax. Once I stopped worrying about what the reader would think of my writing, I could free write and come up with so many more ideas than before. Gabrielle helped me push my limitations. When I first sat down with her to start writing, she gave me a paper and pen and told me to just free write about an important experience of mine. That shocked me big time. I was all, "You're not going to read this, right?" and she was all, "Oh, yes I am. Get to it." Frankly, it was terrifying to let someone in on my first thoughts without preparation. My first thoughts are messy and not very descriptive or profound. But Gabby taught me that that's where you start. She taught me that, in fact, the raw, disorganized memories or ideas are sometimes the most important reflections to get down on paper. Good writing isn't just the refinement of grammar and word choice. It is what blossoms from the core of what you are trying to convey, and sometimes that core is unrefined. But it is powerful.

I learned that it can be painfully difficult to share with someone that your initial thoughts and perceptions are not as refined or even as complete as you like to pretend they are. But I also learned that this is not important. *How you come across as a writer is to be determined in the later stages, and the key is to reflect upon the spirit of your piece.*

To the upcoming writers: Be yourself in your writing! The only way to get across what you truly think is to stop thinking about it. Letting someone see your work is one of the scariest things about being a writer, but in my opinion, expressing raw ideas with complete honesty is even scarier. Do it anyway.

I couldn't have said it better myself. Thank you, Talia Bloom.

Good writing blossoms from the core of what you are trying to convey, and sometimes that core is unrefined. But it is powerful.

You may have fear. Do it anyway!

ACKNOWLEDGMENTS

Deep and heartfelt thanks, first and foremost, to Clifford Chase for his support on this project throughout the years, and most recently, for his insightful and meticulous editing. We have helped each other get unstuck in writing and in life more times than I can count. I am so grateful for our friendship.

To my son, Marco, for his patience, good humor, and kindness in supporting me even when dinner kept getting later and later.

Much gratitude to Tracy Atkins, Tanja Prokop, Valerie Bowman, Kathleen Archambeau, Cheryl Severide Arends, David Richo, Dr. Frankie, Simone Noble, and Steven Levine, for your support along the way. I couldn't have done it without you.

To those with whom I've shared the mystery -- thank you for hearing my barbaric yawp in the wilderness at the moments I needed it most, and encouraging me to write this book.

ABOUT GABRIELLE GLANCY

Former Admissions Director, Series Editor of *Best College Essays*, published in *The New Yorker,* featured on *NPR* and in *USA Today* and author of *The Art of the College Essay,* New Vision Learning's Gabrielle Glancy has been in the business of helping students realize their dreams for over thirty years. With a knack for knowing just the right formula to help high school students succeed where they have struggled and get in where they want to go, she is one of the foremost professionals in her field. Headquartered in Ojai, California, Gabrielle Glancy is well-known all around the world for her college admissions expertise.

Made in the USA
Monee, IL
10 April 2021

65330940R00122